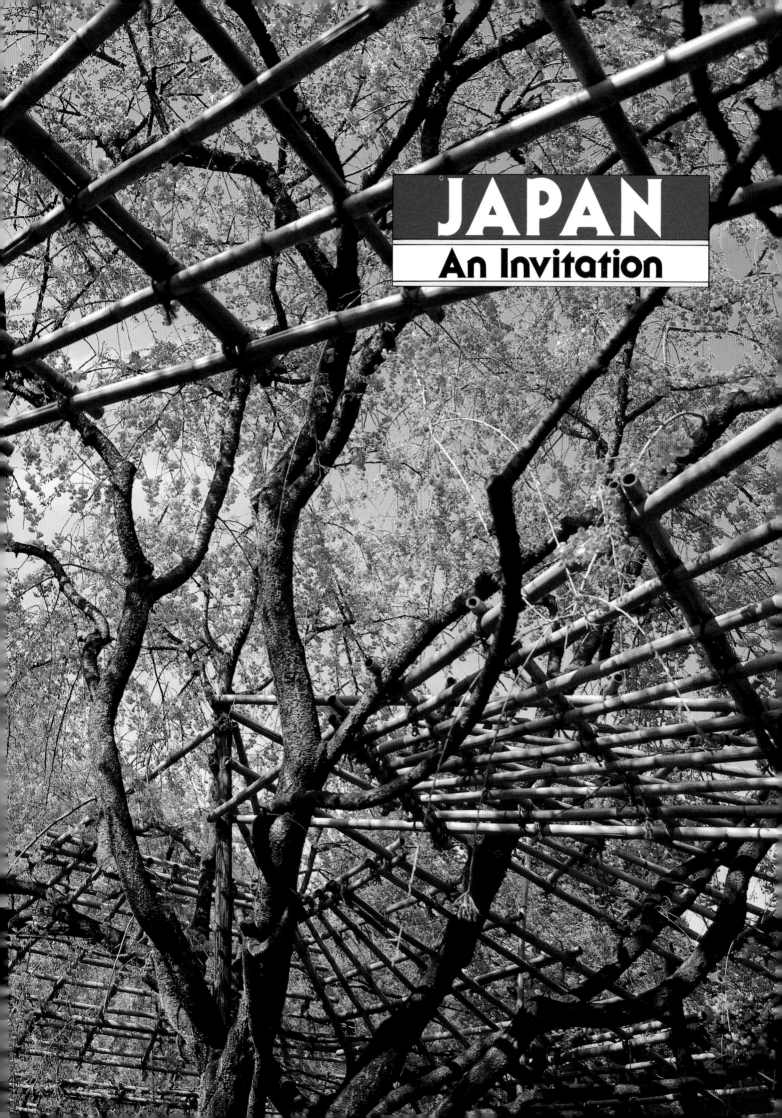

JAPAN
An Invitation

Charles E. Tuttle Company
Tokyo, Japan & Rutland, Vermont

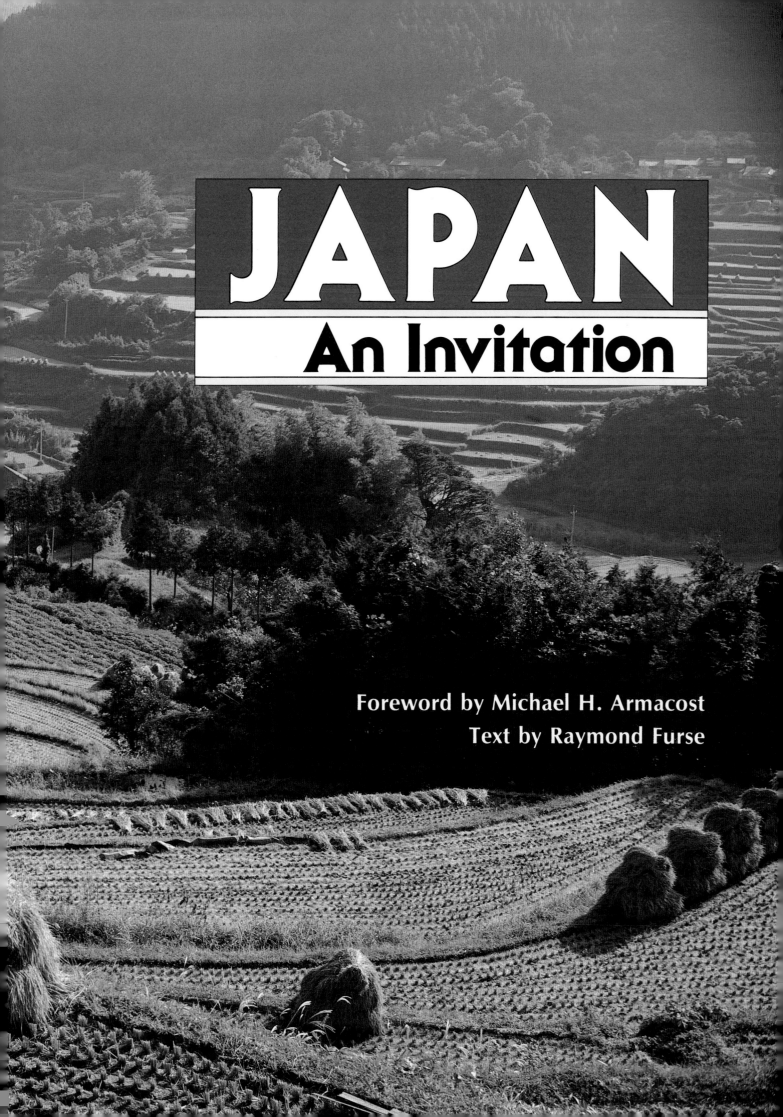

JAPAN
An Invitation

Foreword by Michael H. Armacost
Text by Raymond Furse

Published by the Charles E. Tuttle Company, Inc.
of Rutland, Vermont & Tokyo, Japan
with editorial offices
at 2-6 Suido 1-chome, Bunkyo-ku, Tokyo 112

© 1991 by Charles E. Tuttle Publishing Co., Inc.

Library of Congress Catalog Card No. 91-075849
International Standard Book No. 0-8048-1702-2

First edition, 1991

Printed in Japan

CONTENTS

NOTE: Japanese names follow the traditional order, surname first; others follow Western order. Macrons are used to indicate long vowels in Japanese words, except in proper nouns.

FOREWORD

Michael H. Armacost, United States Ambassador to Japan

Ask a Japanese in English to tell you what is special about his or her country, or what values Japan should share with the world, and he or she may parry the question or express a measure of diffidence. She might suggest the tea ceremony; he might mention diligence or "fighting spirit." Typically Japanese seem uncomfortable explaining their society to outsiders.

Yet it takes little more than a few hours in Japan to recognize this country's special qualities. It is unique not for being an economic powerhouse, which is well known, but in its mood of endeavor, perseverance, and commitment to excellence that is reflected in its approach to business, arts, and sports, as well as its quest for a humane and harmonious society.

What is it about the country that sustains so many traditional arts and crafts? Judo and aikido as well as tea ceremony and Zen meditation, kendo as well as go, Kabuki as well as Noh, ikebana as well as bonsai. A country whose symbol is the immortal Mount Fuji, yet one that prizes ephemeral beauty above all, whether it be in the cherry blossom, the swing of a baseball bat, the vivid impressions of haiku or *tanka,* the morning dew, or the collision of two sumo giants.

The Japanese people's energy is relentless, yet it is matched by their reverence for delicacy, whether in traditional homes made of paper and wood, in woodblock prints, or in lighter-than-air melodies on traditional instruments like the *shamisen* and *koto.*

Ask a Japanese *in Japanese* what is special about Japan, and he or she will feel much more confident—not least because the language welcomes ambiguity of expression. They are likely to refer to *gimu, giri,* or *wa:* duty, responsibility, or cooperation and consideration of others. These treasured values help explain why Japanese streets are so safe, why poverty and social conflicts are relatively rare. At the same time, they also highlight the difficulties the Japanese have sometimes had in coming to grips with the outside world.

This book is designed to help break down Japan's isolation which, while providing the fertile ground for the development of a singular culture, has also complicated its relationships with neighbors, near and more distant.

To live in Japan and observe this society firsthand is to realize that criticisms of Japan are often exaggerated. This nation widely regarded as insular is looking outward, as it has many times in the past. Japanese not only listen to foreign criticisms, but make some of their own, both of their own country and foreign ones too. More and more, the average Japanese supports openness in the economy and genuine cooperation with foreign countries. The word "internationalization," which has caught the fancy of scholars here, has come to embrace all kinds of measures to widen horizons and expand contacts.

There is a much greater effort to try to balance relations with the world, to reach out as well as to take in. Japan is striving to become an import superpower as well as an export titan. This push for balance extends beyond the economic arena. For example, Japan plans to increase dramatically the number of foreign exchange students coming to the archipelago. Moreover, Japan is trying to export its technology as extensively as Japanese companies have absorbed it from abroad. Even on a personal level, it appears that Japanese are striving for greater balance in their lives. Young Japanese are more assertive, more concerned about the quality of family life, and less willing to devote their energies and attention so single-mindedly to their jobs.

Similarly, as the domestic attitude of Japanese changes, so does that of their government. I applaud the Japanese government's desire to be more assertive internationally, and its willingness to begin sharing the political risks as well as the financial costs of international cooperation. The Japanese are merging their self-reliant and harmonious domestic traditions with the universal values of freedom and democracy so that they can confidently play a proper leading role in crafting a peaceful world society.

❖ A Variety of Landscape and Climate ❖

The Japanese archipelago stretches from approximately the 20th to the 45th parallels, comparable to the distance from Cuba to Nova Scotia. With the completion of the 34-mile Seikan Tunnel between Hokkaido and Honshu in 1985 and the 5.6-mile Seto-Ohashi Bridge between Shikoku and Honshu in 1988, the four main islands of Japan became linked by surface transportation.

Largest of these islands is **Honshu**. With the most temperate climate and the most arable land, Honshu provides three-quarters of Japan's annual rice yield. Honshu has long been the stage for Japan's historical and cultural development, being the site of the ancient capitals of Nara, Kyoto, and Kamakura, as well as Tokyo, the present center of government and business.

With its frigid climate, the northern island of **Hokkaido** was the last to be settled, although it was, and remains, home to the indigenous Caucasoid people called Ainu. The Japanese seriously began to colonize Hokkaido only after Russia appeared as a threat in 1860 when Vladivostok was settled. Hokkaido today remains far less populated than the other main islands, and is the only part of Japan with broad vistas of pastureland. As well as scenic beauty, the island is rich in minerals, containing all of Japan's mercury and chrome, three-quarters of its natural gas, and half of its coal.

The westernmost main island of **Kyushu** has historically been the conduit for influences from abroad, in ancient times from China and Korea, more recently from the West. Mongol armadas attempting to invade Kyushu in the 13th century were blown back by fierce winds that the Japanese called *kamikaze*, literally "divine winds." During a period of self-imposed isolation, from the mid-17th to the mid-19th centuries, Japan restricted foreign traders to Nagasaki, which became the country's window on the outside world. Known for its beautiful coastline and abundant natural hot springs, Kyushu is also the location of Mount Aso, one of Japan's most active volcanoes.

The smallest of the main islands, **Shikoku**, lies south of western Honshu, across the Inland Sea. This broad waterway, actually five separate seas linked by channels, stretches more than 300 miles and contains more than 600 small islands. Shikoku is noted for its pilgrimage route to 88 temples associated with Kukai, founder of the Shingon sect of Buddhism. Over 100,000 people visit Shikoku annually to make this pilgrimage.

To the southwest of Kyushu lie the tropical **Ryukyu Islands**, of which Okinawa is best known. Another group of islands, the **Ogasawara Islands**, extends due south of central Honshu and includes the southernmost point of Japan, the island of Okinotorishima.

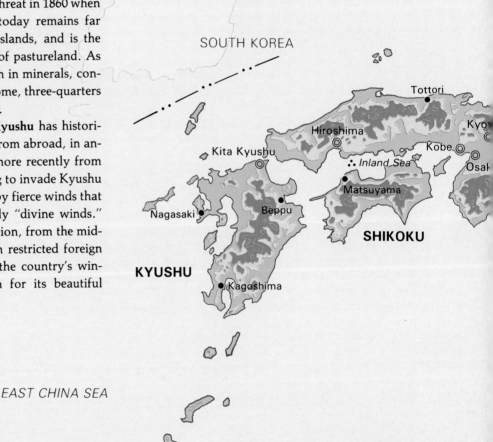

SEA OF JAPAN

SOUTH KOREA

Tottori

Hiroshima

Kita Kyushu

Kobe

Inland Sea

Nagasaki

Beppu

Matsuyama

SHIKOKU

KYUSHU

Kagoshima

CHINA

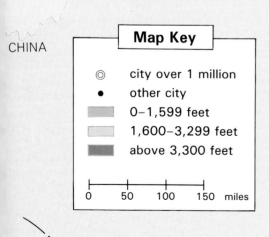

Map Key

◎ city over 1 million
• other city
☐ 0–1,599 feet
☐ 1,600–3,299 feet
☐ above 3,300 feet

0   50   100   150   miles

EAST CHINA SEA

RYUKYU ISLANDS

Naha • Okinawa

TAIWAN

Tropical beach, Ryukyu Islands

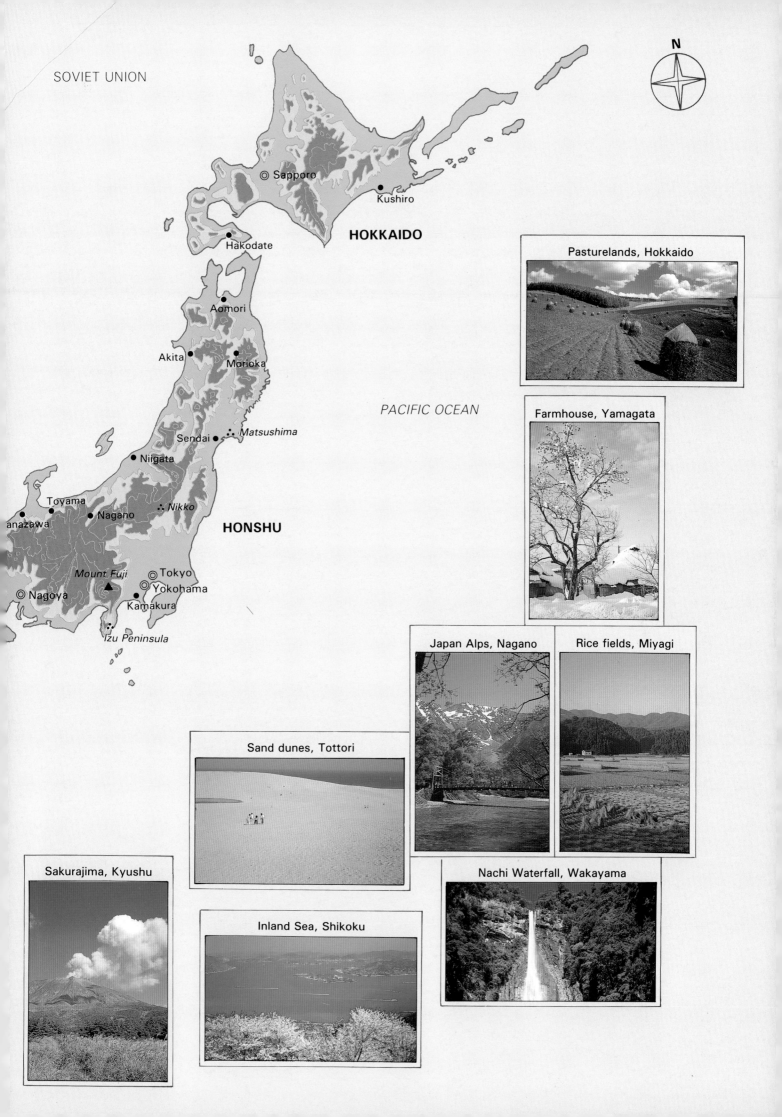

SOVIET UNION

N

◎ Sapporo

● Kushiro

HOKKAIDO

● Hakodate

● Aomori

● Akita

● Morioka

PACIFIC OCEAN

Sendai ● ∴ *Matsushima*

● Niigata

Toyama ●

anazawa ● Nagano ● ∴ *Nikko*

HONSHU

Mount Fuji ▲ ◎ Tokyo
◎ Yokohama
◎ Nagoya ● Kamakura

∴ *Izu Peninsula*

Pasturelands, Hokkaido

Farmhouse, Yamagata

Japan Alps, Nagano

Rice fields, Miyagi

Sand dunes, Tottori

Nachi Waterfall, Wakayama

Sakurajima, Kyushu

Inland Sea, Shikoku

LIVES SHAPED BY MOUNTAINS AND SEAS

Sansui, *a compound of the characters for mountain and water, means landscape or scenery. The word also calls to mind Japan itself, a mountainous country blessed with abundant water resources.*

MOST PEOPLE who have read anything at all about Japan are familiar with the basic facts: Japan is a small, island nation, mountainous and poor in natural resources, populated by a racially homogenous people who speak a common language. These superficially factual notions have been set forth by both Japanese and non-Japanese, and have become widely disseminated and accepted. The problem with such conventional thinking, as with all stereotypes, is that it obscures a reality much more complex and far more interesting.

Japan is indeed a small country. With an area of 145,800 square miles, Japan is smaller than California and a bit larger than Germany. However, its islands extend nearly 2,000 miles from north to south, comparable to the distance from the Canadian border to the tip of Florida. This geographic spread gives Japan a climatic diversity unmatched in countries of comparable size. Although their precise origins remain unclear, the

Left Japan's nearly 17,000 miles of coastline include navigable gulfs and bays as well as rugged and majestic stretches, such as Iwate Prefecture's Rikuchu coast.

Japanese have developed a rich and diverse culture that is clearly a blend of East Asian, Polynesian, and now Western influences. While it is true that the Japanese for the most part are ethnically and linguistically homogenous, geographical and climatic diversity, together with the twin barriers of mountains and seas, have divided the country into distinct regions with differing lifestyles, foods, dialects, and craft traditions.

A mythological account of the creation of the Japanese islands is recorded in Japan's oldest existing chronicle, the *Kojiki* (Record of Ancient Matters), completed in A.D. 712. According to this source, the deities Izanagi and Izanami stood upon the Floating Bridge of Heaven and dipped a jeweled spear into the ocean that covered the world below. Brine dripping from the spear created an island to which the gods descended and made love; their offspring became the other major islands.

The geological account of the formation of the Japanese islands is less romantic, although no less interesting. It is generally agreed that in geological terms they have not long been islands, but at one time formed a mountain range on the eastern rim of the Asian continent, joined at the north to Siberia and at the south to Korea, with the Sea of Japan a huge inland lake. Upthrusting mountains and subsiding seabeds separated this range from the mainland and the individual islands from each other, perhaps as recently as 20,000 years ago.

This cataclysmic geological rearrangement attests to Japan's precarious location on what is colorfully termed the Pacific Fire Ring, a line of intense seismic activity that circles the Pacific Ocean. Japan has more than 40 active volcanoes, and several hundred more have been active in recent history. No one is more aware than the Japanese of the fragility of the cool crust that covers our earth's molten interior. Natural thermal springs abound, and scores of tourist spots feature bubbling pools or jets of sulfurous steam shooting from the ground. Earthquakes, from minor tremors to prolonged, window-rattling shakes, are common occurrences; nearly a tenth of the energy released in the world each year by earthquakes is concentrated in or around Japan.

Located in the temperate monsoon zone of East Asia, Japan is also strongly influenced by seasonal weather patterns. In winter, cold winds blow eastward off the Asian continent, dropping heavy snowfalls on the Sea of Japan side of the islands, while the Pacific coastal side, protected by the high central mountains, enjoys clear skies and moderate temperatures. In summer, warm winds blowing northward from the South Pacific bring typhoons and heavy rains, especially to the southern regions of the country. The transitions between summer and winter also bring rain, especially the long wet season in late spring known as *tsuyu*, literally "plum rains."

Together these geological and environmental factors played a large part in shaping the society, culture, and beliefs of the Japanese. The desirability and necessity of harmony with nature permeated every aspect of Japanese life, and these attitudes are clearly manifested in the rituals and beliefs of the indigenous religion of Shinto. Literally the "way of the gods," Shinto posits the existence of *kami*, deities resident in almost every unusual or prominent natural feature—mountains and rivers, even large trees and rocks. These spirits must be appeased through offerings of rice and saké, and entertained with dances and festivals. Above all, Shinto reveres fertility and purity, both closely associated with water, a resource with which Japan is abundantly blessed. Flowing mountain streams symbolize the flow of human existence, and the power of water to bring life to the rice paddies is readily apparent. The ocean, identified as the source of life in the myth of Izanagi and Izanami, also provides food. The warm Japan Current and the cold Okhotsk Current meet off the coast of Japan, creating extremely fertile fishing grounds. This abundant supply of seafood, along with the Buddhist taboo on eating meat, has resulted in Japan's having the highest per capita consumption of marine products in the world.

Japan's geographical position as an island at the periphery of the Chinese cultural orbit has also been an important factor in its cultural shaping. When China's influence was strong, channels of communication were open, and the Japanese engaged in wholesale cultural borrowing. Conversely, when China was weak, intercourse was disrupted, and Japan returned to being insular and isolationist. During the periods of borrowing, the Japanese showed little regard for the consequences of integrating outside influences into their own culture; periods of isolation, on the other hand, were characterized by reworking and adaptation, making what was borrowed not only harmonize with what was indigenous, but making it *become* Japanese.

The same waves of borrowing and assimilation have characterized Japan's relations with the West, and have given rise to the observation that the Japanese at times appear slavishly imitative, while at other times seem chauvinistically aloof. This reasoning has been extended to explain perceived alternating attitudes of inferiority and superiority toward foreigners. These observations may be useful in helping us form a mental image of the Japanese, but upon close examination, they do little more than describe the broad range of emotional responses that any close-knit community might have toward outsiders. The Japanese, like all nationalities, are products of hereditary and environmental factors. To the extent that these shaping factors are complex, interesting, and unique, so are the Japanese.

Left In mountainous Japan, terraced fields are used for a variety of crops, including rice, tea, and even potatoes, growing here near Uwajima, Ehime Prefecture.

Upper right Solidified lava flows have now joined Sakurajima, an active volcano in Kagoshima Bay, to the rest of Kyushu.

Upper middle right Kobe, Hyogo Prefecture, is typical of many Japanese port cities in that it is tightly nestled between mountains and the sea. Kobe's port has modern harbor facilities capable of handling over 10,000 vessels annually.

Lower middle right Nagano Prefecture, located in the middle of the Japan Alps, is known as the Roof of Japan.

Lower right Although Japan is one of the world's most densely populated nations, the northern island of Hokkaido retains wide-open spaces.

Above Rice farmers in Miyagi Prefecture tend their fields in late summer. Although per capita consumption continues to decrease, rice remains a dietary staple.

Above A Hokkaido fisherwoman strips a net of small walleye, destined for use in fish cakes called kamaboko.

Below Office workers discuss a new project. A strong sense of group loyalty leads to teamwork at the workplace, from the assembly line to the boardroom.

Right A saké maker lifts the steaming rice that is the main ingredient of Japan's national drink. Quality saké is said to have five major characteristics: sweetness, sourness, pungency, bitterness, and astringency.

◈ A HISTORICAL PERSPECTIVE ◈

Japan's history is not accorded importance in the West commensurate with Japan's importance to the West. This neglect is unfortunate, obviously, because Westerners are ignoring a useful tool for understanding the Japanese. It is doubly unfortunate because Westerners are also missing out on a good story. The history of Japan is an ancient and fascinating one, replete with stories of nobility and baseness, triumph and tragedy, romance and adventure. Its heroes and villains, their successes and failures, we can readily understand and marvel at, despite a lack of shared cultural values and traditions.

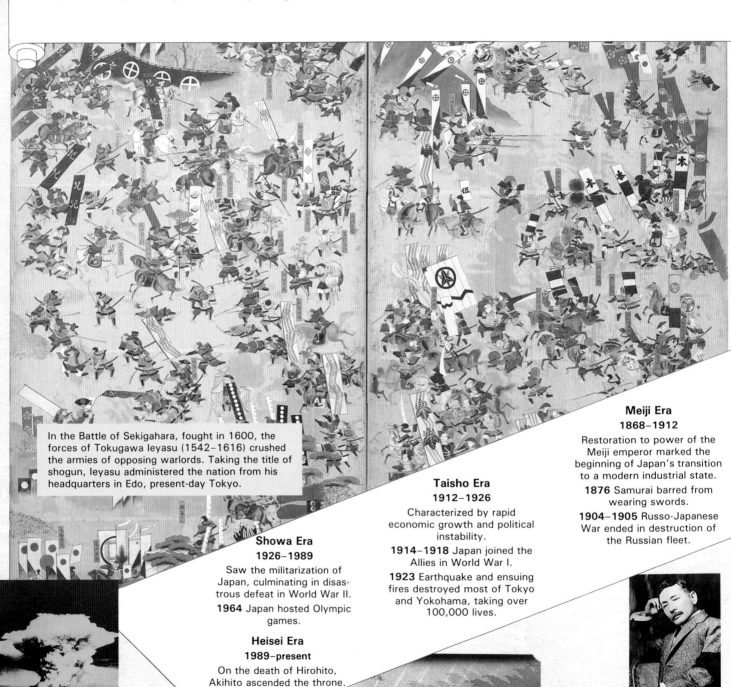

In the Battle of Sekigahara, fought in 1600, the forces of Tokugawa Ieyasu (1542–1616) crushed the armies of opposing warlords. Taking the title of shogun, Ieyasu administered the nation from his headquarters in Edo, present-day Tokyo.

Meiji Era
1868–1912
Restoration to power of the Meiji emperor marked the beginning of Japan's transition to a modern industrial state.
1876 Samurai barred from wearing swords.
1904–1905 Russo-Japanese War ended in destruction of the Russian fleet.

Taisho Era
1912–1926
Characterized by rapid economic growth and political instability.
1914–1918 Japan joined the Allies in World War I.
1923 Earthquake and ensuing fires destroyed most of Tokyo and Yokohama, taking over 100,000 lives.

Showa Era
1926–1989
Saw the militarization of Japan, culminating in disastrous defeat in World War II.
1964 Japan hosted Olympic games.

Heisei Era
1989–present
On the death of Hirohito, Akihito ascended the throne.

Many works of Natsume Soseki (1867–1916), one of Japan's most famous writers, have been translated into English.

The well-known print *Rain at Shono* is from the series *Fifty-three Stages of the Tokaido* by Ando Hiroshige (1797–1858).

The atomic bomb that exploded over Hiroshima on August 6, 1945, eventually killed over 200,000 people.

Yayoi pottery often depicted people and animals.

The figurine called *Venus of Jomon*, at 10.6 inches tall, was larger than most and probably prized.

A great statesman of the Asuka period, Prince Shotoku (574–622) was active as a government administrator, political theorist, and promoter of Buddhism.

Jomon Period
ca. 8000–300 B.C.

Neolithic hunters and gatherers made rope-patterned pottery.

660 B.C. Traditional date of accession of first emperor, Jimmu.

Yayoi Period
ca. 300 B.C.–A.D. 300

Agriculturalists forged tools and made pottery on a wheel.

A.D. 57 First recorded Japanese mission to China.

Tumulus Period
ca. 300–552

Dominated by a martial dynasty; named for massive burial mounds.

Asuka Period
552–710

Extensive revision of laws and regulations, based on Buddhism and Confucianism.

552 Buddhism introduced into Japan.

Nara Period
710–794

Court moved to Heijokyo (now Nara), a new capital modeled on the Chinese capital at Changan.

712 *Kojiki* (Record of Ancient Matters) compiled.

720 *Nihon Shoki* (Chronicle of Japan) compiled.

752 Great Buddha at Nara dedicated.

Heian Period
794–1185

Institution of the court reached its zenith during the period, which saw a flourishing of art and high culture.

794 Emperor Kammu established new capital in Heian-kyo (now Kyoto).

ca. 1015 *The Tale of Genji*, the world's first novel, completed.

Minamoto no Yoritomo (1147–1199) led the campaigns in which his Minamoto clan defeated its arch-enemy, the Taira. Yoritomo was the first to take the title of shogun, initiating seven centuries of feudal warrior-government rule.

Kamakura Period
1185–1336

A new warrior class came to power, with the shogun ruling in the name of the emperor.

1192 Yoritomo became shogun.

1281 An invading Mongol force of 140,000 men destroyed in a furious storm called *kamikaze*, literally "divine winds."

Muromachi Period
1336–1568

Marked by weak central government and incessant warfare but flourishing art and technology.

1338 Ashikaga family gained control of Japan and moved shogunate to the Muromachi district in Kyoto.

Azuchi-Momoyama Period 1568–1600

Called Japan's Age of Grandeur because of cultural achievements, the period was marked by civil war.

1582 Oda Nobunaga (1534–1582), having just won control of central Japan, committed hara-kiri when betrayed by his own vassal.

Tokugawa (Edo) Period 1600–1868

For much of the period, contact with outsiders banned, except with Dutch at Nagasaki.

1603 Tokugawa family of shoguns gained control of the government.

1853 Commodore Perry and his "black ships" arrived to forcibly open Japan.

Daily life at the Heian court at its zenith, shown here in *Lady Murasaki's Diary Scroll*, saw a preoccupation with the minutest details of cultural, aesthetic, and ceremonial matters. The period also witnessed the transition from the wholesale adoption of Chinese models to the development of a distinct and highly refined Japanese culture.

Nagasaki was first opened to the outside world in 1571, initially as a trading post with the Portuguese, later with the Chinese, English, and Dutch. The screen shows a Japanese painter's exaggerated portrait of foreigners wearing strange hats and baggy pants.

THE YAMATO NATION

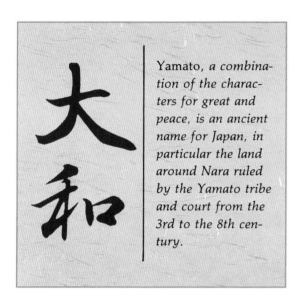

Yamato, *a combination of the characters for great and peace, is an ancient name for Japan, in particular the land around Nara ruled by the Yamato tribe and court from the 3rd to the 8th century.*

ACCORDING TO ancient chronicles, the largest of the islands created by the gods Izanagi and Izanami was dubbed Yamato. Amaterasu, the Sun Goddess, later dispatched her grandson Ninigi to rule over this land, bestowing upon him three symbols of divine authority: a mirror, sword, and jewels, regalia which are still identified with the imperial family. Ninigi's grandson Jimmu finally succeeded in conquering Yamato, ascending the earthly throne in 660 B.C. While Jimmu may have been an actual historical personage, it is certain that this account of his deeds was fabricated at a much later date, probably to endow Japan with an antiquity comparable to that of neighboring China.

The original meaning of the name Yamato is unclear; one theory is that it derives from the Japanese for "mountain gate." The name probably first designated a single tribe or village in western Honshu, only later coming to be applied to the entire island, and finally to all of Japan

Left Kyoto's Aoi Matsuri, which originated in the 7th century, features ox-driven carriages, a means of transportation for the nobility of the Heian period.

as more and more territory was brought under control. The mid-6th century B.C. marks the verifiable, rather than the mythical, ascendancy of the Yamato tribe. Nevertheless, the true origins of this people, the forebears of today's Japanese, remain obscure.

The earliest inhabitants of Japan were Paleolithic groups that wandered into the area when it was joined to the mainland during the last glacial age. Although it is certain that the Japanese are a Mongoloid race, ethnically related to other East Asians, many cultural elements, among them architectural styles and the myth of the Sun Goddess as divine progenitrix, point to strong Polynesian influences.

Japan's earliest people were capable of shaping crude stone implements but were unable to make pottery. Sometime around 8000 B.C. Japan's inhabitants evolved from a "nonpottery" people to a Neolithic people able to make pottery that is impressed with rope patterns. The Japanese term for this distinctive pottery lends its name to the period, the Jomon, which lasted until around 300 B.C.

The Yayoi period that followed marked another distinct cultural shift. While Jomon pottery was shaped, Yayoi pottery was turned on a wheel. Jomon people were nomadic hunters and gatherers, while Yayoi people were wet-rice farmers who were able to forge tools and weapons of bronze and iron.

Wet-rice farming demands intensive labor, organization, and cooperation, and it is credited with fostering the values of diligence, loyalty, and group cohesion often remarked as characteristic of modern Japanese. It is not certain whether this shift from hunters and gatherers to farmers was due to the natural evolution of a single people or to new migrations from outside of Japan.

The 4th century A.D. marks the beginning of the Tumulus period, so named for the enormous burial mounds that are its archaeological legacy. The largest of these, located near Osaka, dates from the 5th century and is about 1,600 feet long. Pottery called *haniwa*,

many pieces simple cylinders but others depicting warriors, houses, horses, and other animals, was often arranged around the mounds. It has been suggested that these mound builders were tribes of mounted warriors from the mainland who conquered Japan around A.D. 300, and the similarity of their tomb designs to those of Korea and China lends support to this theory. However, the mounds might also be the work of the highly organized Yamato tribes under the sway of styles from the Asian mainland, with which there was ongoing contact.

Because it is thought that mound building may have ceased due to Buddhist influence, the year 552, the traditional date of the introduction of Buddhism into Japan, is used to mark the end of the Tumulus period. By this time, the Yamato people had conquered much of what is modern Japan (though northern Honshu and Hokkaido remained under control of the Ainu, an indigenous Caucasoid race). The land was administered by *uji*, clans headed by hereditary chieftains and ranked hierarchically under the leading Yamato tribe. The emperor was not yet the divine descendant that later histories were to designate him, but simply the head of the ruling *uji*.

Yamato people were believers in Shinto, a religion whose most important monument is the Grand Shrine at Ise, said to date from the 3rd century A.D. and to enshrine the Sun Goddess, who is represented by the same sacred mirror she bestowed upon Ninigi. Ise Shrine is constructed of unpainted cypress, and since antiquity has been rebuilt about every 20 years in adjacent, alternating sites. The clean lines and unadorned wood of Ise exemplify the aesthetic preference for naturalness, while the ritual rebuilding reflects the Japanese value of purity and belief in the possibility of spiritual renewal.

As were previous influences from the mainland, Buddhism was initially well received at the Yamato court. However, its premise—to transcend this world of pain and suffering through meditation, study, and ascetic practices—was at variance with the Shinto focus on the joyous celebration of nature and fertility here and now. By the end of the 6th century, clashes were breaking out between factions favoring acceptance of the new religion and others opposing it. Buddhism eventually won acceptance, perhaps less because of its message than because it was the religion of the country that at the time possessed the highest culture in the world, China of the Tang dynasty.

The 6th century marked the beginning of another round of massive cultural borrowing from the mainland, a trend that was to characterize the next 300 years, shaping and transforming areas such as art, education, architecture, religion, and politics. The written language of China was adopted, paving the way to the development of a literary tradition. Japanese monks visiting China returned bearing not only Buddhist texts and

Above *Meotoiwa, the "wedded rocks" near Ise, are joined by a rope and symbolize the male and female deities Izanagi and Izanami, the mythical creators of Japan.*

Below *In the* namahage, *an ancient New Year's rite still observed with gusto in Akita Prefecture, young men dressed as ogres visit neighborhood homes, warning against laziness in the coming year.*

Above The public greets Emperor Akihito and his family at the Imperial Palace in Tokyo.

Right These dancers are one of the many types of haniwa, *earthenware objects that decorated or guarded ancient burial mounds.*

philosophical ideas, but also Chinese concepts of temple architecture and urban design.

The Asuka period, from 552 to 710, saw an extensive revision of Japanese laws and regulations that was based on Buddhist and Confucian precepts. Credit for these innovations is historically accorded Prince Shotoku, who remains an important cultural hero. It is likely, however, that many of these important changes were brought on by pro-Buddhist clan leaders, particularly Umako, head of the powerful Soga *uji,* who reinstituted embassies to China in the early 7th century.

The Yamato court made it clear to the Chinese that it did not accept the subordinate status normally associated with countries that sent tribute missions. About this same time, the court began to refer to the area under its political control as Nippon, using two Chinese characters meaning "source of the sun." The new name affirmed Japan's location to the east of China, and, consequently, its position as the origin of the heavenly body that illuminated the civilized world. It is the corrupted Chinese pronunciation of the Chinese characters that gives the English "Japan." At this time also, the term *tennō*, or "heavenly sovereign," was adopted to refer to the ruler of Yamato, according him the divine status enjoyed by the Chinese emperor.

It is clear that whoever the Yamato people were, these ancestors of the Japanese were not a monocultural and monoracial people developing in isolation. On the contrary, they were a dynamic and highly organized group of tribes, whose culture was the result of successive waves of immigrants and influences from both the East Asian mainland and the Pacific islands. Even at this early stage, they exhibited traits often observed in modern Japanese—the ability to draw from a wide variety of artistic styles, administrative methods, and belief systems, and to adapt and implement these to meet their specific needs.

Right *Symbol of Japan and sacred to both Buddhist and Shinto adherents, Mount Fuji rises 12,385 feet and forms one of the world's finest volcanic cones. During the summer months, tens of thousands of people climb the famous mountain.*

◈ EMBRACING THE SPIRITS ◈

Since antiquity, the Japanese have stood in awe of nature, personified in the *kami* (deities) associated with prominent natural features such as mountains and rivers. Ensuring harmony between these powers and mankind required the proper seasonal rituals of purification, fertility, and thanksgiving. These were the responsibility of the Shinto priesthood. Initially a loosely structured assemblage of local myths, creeds, and practices, Shinto became more organized and its rituals more codified during the 8th and 9th centuries, as it was forced to compete for support with Buddhism. However, the two belief systems managed to coexist and interact, spawning a variety of syncretic sects and doctrines. Important religious complexes usually included both Shinto and Buddhist places of worship. It was not until the Meiji Restoration in 1868 that Shinto was purged of its Buddhist associations and its position as the orthodox state religion confirmed.

Still, the Japanese have never felt the need to adhere to the doctrine of any specific sect or faith, preferring to satisfy their spiritual requirements through whatever course seems customary and plausible. Weddings are predominantly held under Shinto auspices, while Buddhist rites seem more appropriate for funerals. This reflects Shinto's traditional concern with fertility and its abhorrence of death, as well as Buddhism's preoccupation with the problems of rebirth and spiritual growth. For many other rites of passage, however, such as finding a spouse, passing an important examination, or getting a good job, one might turn to either creed for help. Perhaps because of this approach to religion, Christianity never made great inroads in Japan, for it demanded that the Japanese choose its doctrine over those of native offerings, while failing to address a spiritual need that was not already being provided for.

The Shinto Shrine

By convention, Shinto places of worship are called shrines in English, while those of Buddhism are referred to as temples. A distinctive and pervasive feature of shrine architecture is the torii, *the tiered gateway that serves to separate sacred precincts from the mundane world, and through which devotees and visitors usually pass to reach the buildings within. Although many* torii *are painted an auspicious vermilion, others are fashioned of plain, unfinished beams.*

Unusual natural features on the grounds or in the neighborhood are thought to have a special relationship with the shrine and its tutelary deities. An ancient or huge tree, for example, may be designated a shinboku, *literally a "god tree." Such natural features are typically adorned with* shimenawa *(sacred ropes of twisted straw) from which strips of white paper are hung. These Shinto symbols of purity are also seen above the entrances to shrine buildings and serve, as do* torii, *to demarcate the sacred.*

Overseeing the various rites of the shrine is the kannushi *(chief priest).* Miko *(shrine maidens) assist the priests in their ceremonial functions and on special occasions perform dances to sacred music.*

The Buddhist Temple

Japanese temple architecture has been strongly influenced by both Korean and Chinese models. Often seen on temple grounds is a pagoda, a multistory tower where sacred relics are enshrined.

The largest and most central building on the temple grounds is usually the hondō (main hall), where images of the principal deities are kept and services are held. Besides being places of worship, temples generally serve as quarters for nuns and monks. Their activities include overseeing services, engaging in ascetic practices, and studying Buddhist scriptures. A bell to mark the times for daily observances and repositories for scriptures or treasures are also typical temple features.

In both the Shinto and Buddhist faiths, regular attendance at worship services is not customary; however, Japanese typically make visits to shrines and temples throughout the year for private reasons or on special occasions. Conducted with sincerity and appropriate demeanor, such visits are considered acts of worship.

Below The historical accommodation of Shinto and Buddhism is seen at Itsukushima, Hiroshima Prefecture. According to tradition, the shrine is dedicated to daughters of Susanoo, the sister of the sun goddess in the Shinto pantheon, but for centuries the chief shrine deity was the Buddhist goddess of fortune. Architectural evidence of this Shinto-Buddhist syncretism is seen in the torii and the five-story pagoda.

THE ANCIENT CAPITALS

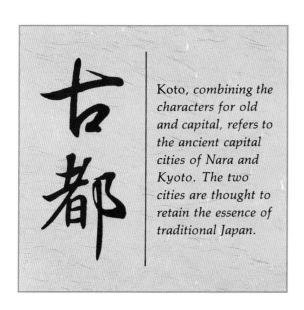

Koto, *combining the characters for old and capital, refers to the ancient capital cities of Nara and Kyoto. The two cities are thought to retain the essence of traditional Japan.*

KYOTO AND NARA, two ancient cities just 40 miles apart, are together considered the cultural center of Japan. Kyoto, the country's capital for over a thousand years, is the embodiment of Japanese traditions, for it was here, during the golden age of court life, that Japanese art and aesthetics developed. Nara lays claim to the title of the nation's spiritual center, for it was here that Buddhism was first practiced in Japan. The streets, architecture, gardens, and museums of both Kyoto and Nara are steeped in history, and it is fortunate indeed that these two cities were spared bombing during World War II. Nowhere else does Japan's rich and varied past reveal itself so clearly.

During their 5th- and 6th-century conquest of Japan, the Yamato clans frequently changed the location of their headquarters. These moves were probably dictated by a strategic consideration, the need to keep political authority close to the areas of military concentration. By

Left The three-story pagoda of Kiyomizudera in Kyoto, a temple complex first established in 798, is dedicated to Kannon, the Buddhist deity of compassion.

the 8th century, however, Yamato territory was sufficiently secure to allow a permanent capital, and in 710 the court was moved to Heijokyo, now called Nara.

At this time, Chinese cultural influence was particularly strong, and the new city was laid out in a grid pattern in imitation of the Chinese capital of Changan (modern Xian). China, under the Tang dynasty, controlled the silk routes linking Asia with the Middle East and Europe, and intercourse with Japan extended these routes eastward. Nara became a cosmopolitan urban center, with visitors from all over Asia arriving with exotic wares and new ideas.

The Nara period saw the birth of Japanese literature. The great historical accounts of Japan, the *Kojiki* (Record of Ancient Matters) and *Nihon Shoki* (Chronicle of Japan), were compiled in 712 and 720 respectively. Also compiled during the Nara period was the *Manyōshū* (Collection of Ten Thousand Leaves), the first anthology of Japanese poetry, containing over 4,500 poems in a variety of styles.

Itinerant Buddhist monks returned to Japan with the texts and doctrines of the mainland sects, and established grand temples in the new capital. State sponsorship of Buddhism led to the construction of sprawling Todaiji, a temple complex boasting the largest wooden building in the world. Todaiji houses a great bronze Buddha 53 feet tall, which was dedicated in 752 in a ceremony witnessed by Buddhist clergy from as far away as India. Another surviving structure originally part of the Todaiji complex is Shosoin, a warehouse containing more than 10,000 items dating from the 8th century, treasures brought to Japan from the far corners of the then civilized world, including Assyria, Arabia, Persia, Greece, Rome, and Egypt. The grounds of Kofukuji, another of the so-called Seven Great Temples of Nara, contain a magnificent five-story pagoda, first built in 730. Destroyed five times by fire, it was last rebuilt, to the original specifications, in 1426.

These designated National Treasures still stand today,

clustered about Nara Park at the city center. With its huge cedars, oaks, and wisteria, this 1,300-acre stretch of rolling green is popularly known as Deer Park, as more than one thousand tame deer are allowed to roam freely through it. To the southwest of the city is Horyuji, dating from the Asuka period (mid-6th century to 710). Built in 607 by Prince Shotoku, Horyuji is the oldest surviving temple in Japan, and its main hall and five-story pagoda are among the oldest wooden buildings in the world. With a population of a third of a million, modern Nara is the home of some of the nation's greatest treasures, and is still considered the cradle of Japanese civilization.

Above Designed by Muromachi landscape artist Soami (ca. 1455–1525), the austere and enigmatic stone garden of Ryoanji in Kyoto contains only 15 oddly shaped stones arranged in a sea of raked, white sand.

Left A maiko (apprentice geisha) steps into the streets of the Gion district, the geisha quarters of Kyoto. A knowledge of Japanese classical dance and music is a necessity for geisha, members of a respected and enduring tradition.

By the end of the 8th century, the powerful Buddhist establishment in Nara was thought to be meddling excessively in government affairs, and in 784 Emperor Kammu elected to move the court to a splendid new capital called Heiankyo, present-day Kyoto, also built according to a Chinese grid plan. During the 300 years of the Heian period, the institution of the court reached its cultural zenith while, concurrently, the imperial house experienced an erosion of political power. At this time, the Fujiwara clan was beginning its rise to prominence, managing to insinuate its members into many positions of authority, including successive regents to young emperors. The authority of the Fujiwara regents was to last into the 11th century, establishing a line of emperors who reigned but did not rule, titular sovereigns who relied on a powerful nobility to administer the nation while they remained withdrawn, preoccupied with aesthetic pursuits and matters of ritual and protocol. The emperors were not overthrown, however, because of the belief that the imperial line was descended directly from the Sun Goddess.

The Heian period saw the flourishing of a native high culture. As increasing turmoil on the mainland diminished the cultural influence of China, the Japanese turned inward, modifying and adapting borrowed aesthetic concepts and artistic traditions to suit their needs. A phonetic script called *kana* was developed which, in conjunction with Chinese characters borrowed earlier, facilitated the task of transcribing Japanese, allowing a vernacular literature to flourish. Admired for its sensitive depiction of court life, *The Tale of Genji*, the world's first novel, was completed shortly after the year 1000. Poetry was in vogue at the court, with courtiers concentrating on the *tanka*, a poem of 31 syllables. Above all, the Heian noble strove to attain a refined elegance, an important component of which was an emotional sensitivity known as *mono no aware*, an appreciation of the ephemeral beauty of life. Acutely aware of the passage of time and the transient nature of all phenomena, the Heian aesthete responded emotionally to the slightest allusion to these inexorable truths in art and literature.

By the 12th century, Fujiwara power at the court had waned, and a struggle for political control was being waged between the powerful Taira clan of Kyoto and the rising Minamoto clan, based on the Kanto Plain. The five-year Taira-Minamoto War between the two clans resulted in the defeat of the Taira in 1185, in the Battle of Dannoura in the seas off Shimonoseki. Minamoto no Yoritomo assumed the title of shogun, or military governor, and ruled Japan from headquarters he established in

Right *The main hall of Sanzen'in, in Kyoto's Ohara district, is considered one of the best remaining examples of 10th-century temple architecture.*

Above *Kinkakuji (Golden Pavilion) was built by the third Ashikaga shogun, Yoshimitsu (1358–1408), as part of his retirement villa. In accordance with his wishes, it was turned into a temple after his death.*

Kamakura, a seaside city near present-day Tokyo. In 1338 the Kamakura shogun was defeated by renegade branches of the Minamoto clan, and the shogunate was reestablished in Kyoto, in a district known as Muromachi.

Although the Muromachi period (1336–1568) was marked by weak central government and incessant warfare, high culture flourished. Many of the arts regarded as those of classical Japan, including ink painting, ikebana, and the Noh drama, were developed or refined during this period. During this time, the austerely elegant rules of the tea ceremony were also codified,

Above *A temple dedicated to the Buddha of healing, Nara's Yakushiji houses several masterpieces of early Nara-period sculpture. The East Pagoda, shown on the right, survives from the 8th century.*

Left *Nara is a popular destination for school excursions. Many of the city's most famous sights are clustered around Nara Park, an oasis of greenery and home of Nara's famous tame deer.*

Preceding pages *The entrance gate to Komyoji, one of Kyoto's more than 1,600 temples, shows Japan's autumn beauty at its finest.*

as was the interior design suitable for the room in which this ritual was held. With its fully tatami-matted floor and decorative alcove, this room became the prototype for the traditional Japanese living room.

As the seat of the emperor and his court for more than a millennium, Kyoto was and continues to be regarded as the repository of Japanese culture and aesthetic traditions. And unlike in Tokyo, the historical monuments and treasures of Kyoto are in evidence everywhere. A modern city of 1.4 million people, Kyoto possesses about 20 percent of Japan's designated National Treasures and 15 percent of the nation's Important Cultural Assets. Over 200 Shinto shrines and approximately 1,600 Buddhist temples are distributed throughout the city. Some of these, like shimmering Kinkakuji (Golden Pavilion), have been destroyed by fire but rebuilt to original specifications with traditional methods of construction. Gardens are another cultural attraction; more than 60 of Japan's loveliest are located in Kyoto, including the elegant moss garden of Saihoji and the enigmatic stone garden of Ryoanji.

Besides being a city of ancient monuments, Kyoto is also a center of traditional crafts. Beautiful silk brocades and other fine fabrics are woven, dyed, and embroidered in Kyoto. Small workshops turning out exquisite ceramics, lacquerware, cloisonné, and folding fans flourish. Moreover, Kyoto celebrates its cultural heritage with numerous annual festivals, including the spectacular Gion Festival, a procession of floats, and the Jidai Festival, a parade of men, women, and children wearing costumes in styles dating back 1,100 years. While Tokyo may thrive as the economic and political center of Japan, to the Japanese, the true soul of the nation is the ancient capital of Kyoto.

Below *Although technically never a capital of Japan, Osaka served as a base of power for Toyotomi Hideyoshi (1537–1598), who subdued rival feudal lords to reunite the nation at the end of the 16th century. Hideyoshi also persuaded the merchants of nearby Sakai and Fushimi to relocate to his new base of power, starting Osaka on the road to its present commercial importance. The castle he built in 1586, although destroyed and rebuilt several times, stands as a symbol of Osaka.*

The natural environment of Japan has played a decisive role in shaping Japanese art and aesthetics. Attuned to the landscape and four distinct seasons of their islands, Japanese artists drew upon nature for their themes and materials. Depictions of pine, plum, chrysanthemum, and cherry appear prominently on lacquerware, ceramics, textiles, and objects fashioned of bamboo, paper, and wood. Especially in painting and poetry, two arts closely linked in the Orient, themes were inevitably of nature or presented through natural motifs.

Believing that the majesty and mystery of nature defied realistic portrayal, Japanese artists came to favor symbolic representation. To reveal the secrets of nature, suggestion was preferred over description, simplicity over ornateness. The refined elegance so highly valued by the Heian court was to be found in the restrained, in the suggestive. The sensitive aesthete was capable of being emotionally moved by a perfect brush stroke or a striking poetic image.

Impermanence was another observable characteristic of nature: what was exquisitely beautiful was readily perishable. An aesthetic appreciation of the evanescent developed, fortified by the Buddhist belief in the impermanence of all things. The Western notion of attaining immortality through art was never popular. Conversely, nature's impermanence was a sanction for imperfection; what was spontaneous, even eccentric, was alive and natural. Thus a tea-ceremony bowl with a flattened side or runny glaze might be praised for its vitality.

Preference for the natural, however, did not restrain the artist from using calculated artifice. Particularly in gardens and flower arrangements, great effort was expended to attain the desired "natural" effect.

Moreover, the artist was never assumed responsible for portraying the more base, perhaps more natural, side of human existence. Until the rise of an urban popular culture in the Edo period, little attempt was made to portray the everyday life of the common people.

IRIS SCREENS, Ogata Korin
(Nezu Museum)
A master of decorative arts, Ogata Korin (1658–1716) applied his talents to textiles, pottery, lacquerware, and screens. Although his sketchbooks show him capable of portraying nature realistically, he is famous for his sug-gestive use of natural motifs. His six-paneled Iris Screens *show green plants with blue blossoms that seem to be dancing on a background of gold leaf, evoking, rather than copying, a natural setting.*

TEABOWL "AMADERA," Chojiro
(Tokyo National Museum)

*Kyoto potter Chojiro (1516–1592) is generally
acknowledged as the originator of Raku ware, a rustic-
looking pottery with strong but simple shapes and rich,
black or red glazes, intended for use in the tea ceremony.
The naturalness of Raku ware's shapes and colors and
the imperfection of the hand-shaped pieces exemplified
spontaneity and unpretentiousness, qualities appreciated
by both the Zen adept and the tea-ceremony master.*

HABOKU LANDSCAPE, Sesshu Toyo
(Tokyo National Museum)

*Regarded by many critics as Japan's greatest painter,
Sesshu Toyo (1420–1506) was influenced by the work of
Chinese Sung and Ming landscape masters. Sesshu's
painting is noted for its dynamic brushwork, as in this
landscape done in* haboku, *or "splashed ink," style.
Although such brief and suggestive portrayals implied
spontaneous execution, in fact, years of study were
required to master the necessary brush techniques.*

LACQUER BOX, Hon'ami Koetsu
(Tokyo National Museum)

*Hon'ami Koetsu (1558–1637) was known for lacquerware
and pottery decorated with his own painting and
calligraphy. This box, intended to hold inkstones, shows
a pontoon bridge arching over golden waters, and is
decorated with a poem.*

THE EASTERN CAPITAL

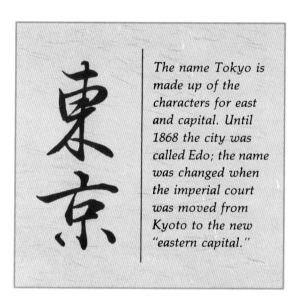

The name Tokyo is made up of the characters for east and capital. Until 1868 the city was called Edo; the name was changed when the imperial court was moved from Kyoto to the new "eastern capital."

ANYONE WISHING to understand Japan must sooner or later come to grips with the astounding megalopolis that is modern Tokyo. Although Japan has ten other cities with populations of over 1 million, Tokyo is unparalleled in terms of wealth, population, modernity, economic importance, and international feeling. It is, after all, a city that stretches over 2,000 square miles, is home to more than 12 million people, and has an annual budget larger than that of China. One can also say that Tokyo best represents modern Japan, for it is the showcase of what the Japanese, for good or bad, are making of their nation.

Tokyo is not an ancient city. Although the Kanto Plain on which it is located was inhabited in prehistoric times, the city's rise to prominence began when Tokugawa Ieyasu established his headquarters there in 1603. Ieyasu, having been granted a domain covering most of the Kanto Plain, built his castle on land that is

Left The sun rises over the skyscrapers of Tokyo, Japan's political and economic center for the past several centuries.

now part of the Imperial Palace grounds; the remains of circular castle moats can still be discerned today. With his resounding defeat of opposing daimyo, or feudal lords, at the Battle of Sekigahara in 1600, Ieyasu succeeded in unifying the nation. He then secured his hold on the country by requiring that daimyo spend alternate years in the new shogunal headquarters and that their heirs and main wives reside there permanently. The districts in which these feudal lords lived are now Tokyo's major business districts (Marunouchi, Otemachi, and Hibiya) and the center of the national government (Kasumigaseki and Nagatacho). In the surrounding lowlands (Kanda, Nihombashi, and Kyobashi) lived the townspeople—merchants, craftsmen, and peasants, who supplied the city with goods, services, and labor.

The success of Ieyasu's military and political strategies ushered in a long period of peace, referred to as either the Tokugawa period or the Edo period, after the city's name at that time. Peace brought growth and prosperity to Edo; in less than a century it became the most populous city in the world, with over a million inhabitants. Ironically, the chief beneficiaries of the new stability were merchants, traditionally the lowest class of society, while, with no battles to fight, the upper-class samurai lost prestige and power.

As the city prospered, the pursuit of pleasure led to the rise of a new, middle-class, urban culture. This culture is reflected in theater arts that thrive today, Kabuki and Noh, as well as in institutions that no longer exist, such as the great pleasure quarters of Yoshiwara. The daily lives of the courtesans, samurai, actors, and artists of old Edo are preserved in *ukiyo-e*, literally "floating-world pictures," the colorful woodblock prints that illustrated popular Edo-period printed matter and now command the prices of fine art. The word *ukiyo-e* derives from a Buddhist term for the underlying insubstantiality of the world we perceive as real and reflects the continuing importance accorded *mono no aware*, the appreciation of the ephemeral beauty of life,

Above *Shinjuku Station is the busiest in Japan, handling more than 2.5 million passengers daily, most of them commuters who live to the west and northwest of Tokyo.*

Below *Portable shrines called* mikoshi *are paraded through the streets in one of Tokyo's biggest festivals, the Sanja Matsuri, held annually in the Asakusa district.*

an aesthetic value since the Heian period. Life was to be experienced or, more precisely, to be emotionally felt; the true *Edokko*, or "child of Edo," was always either spending or, if broke, scheming to get funds for visits to the public baths, the theaters, or the brothel areas.

The evanescence of all things was neither an abstract concept to Edo townspeople nor simply a license for frivolity. It was a hard fact of Edo life, one emphasized repeatedly by both man-made and natural disasters. Most frequent and damaging of these were the fires known popularly as "flowers of Edo." These were usually started by cooking fires that spread due to one of the frequent earthquakes or to simple carelessness, and would blaze out of control in the densely packed neighborhoods of wooden dwellings. A great conflagration in 1657 killed over 100,000 people, at that time more than a quarter of the city's population. Fires and earthquakes, typhoons and floods, and outbreaks of cholera made Edo life extremely precarious. Two events in the mid-19th century, however, ensured that Edo would maintain its economic, cultural, and political sway over the nation. The first was the opening of Japan to the West by Commodore Perry, ending two centuries of self-imposed seclusion. The second was the overthrow of

Tokugawa leadership by a group of younger samurai from western Japan and the restoration of the emperor to political authority. This event, the Meiji Restoration, resulted in the imperial court being moved from Kyoto to Edo, which was then renamed Tokyo, literally "eastern capital."

There is a significant connection between these two events. It was the West's superiority in technology and armaments that allowed it to dictate to Japan the terms of a new relationship. Japan's shortcomings did not escape the notice of those opposing the increasingly weak and conservative Tokugawa authorities. Although the Meiji Restoration appeared to be a return to the prefeudal system of imperial rule, it actually inaugurated the modernization of Japan, which was successfully attained through organized and large-scale borrowing from the West. Within a half century, Japan became militarily powerful enough to defeat Russia and to annex Korea, Taiwan, and the Ryukyu Islands. In the following decades, however, increasing military expansion was to bring Japan into armed conflict with the West.

Tokyo's rapid growth suffered a severe blow with the Tokyo Earthquake of 1923. During the catastrophe, in which fires did more damage than the earthquake itself,

Above *Shibuya, an important transportation center serving the southwestern suburbs of Tokyo, has become a trendy district for shopping and entertainment.*

Below *Seafood for Tokyo's millions of fish lovers passes through the wholesale market at Tsukiji. Sales of Tsukiji's more than 450 varieties of marine products top $5 billion annually.*

Above Although Tokyo has been almost entirely rebuilt over the last five decades, traces remain of the old residential areas, such as this street in the Hongo district.

Below Home of the Tokugawa shoguns for more than two centuries, the grounds of Edo Castle, now the site of the Imperial Palace, are still separated from the rest of the city by moats and high walls.

over 100,000 people died and 60 percent of the homes were destroyed. Although mostly rebuilt by 1930, in 1945 Tokyo suffered another cataclysmic man-made disaster. From January 1945 until the surrender of Japan that August, Tokyo was firebombed over one hundred times, suffering damage comparable to that of its greatest natural disasters. Again, over 100,000 people were killed and most of the city was destroyed. As it had so many times in the past, however, Tokyo quickly rose from its own ashes, adding nearly 5 million residents between 1952, the end of the Occupation, and 1964, the year it arrived as a world-class capital by hosting the Olympic games.

Reflecting its origins and history, modern Tokyo is a city in continuous flux. Its residents seem always on the move and its structures seem to be constantly changing. It is not a city of monuments but of people, who are either hard at work, hard at play, or on their way to do one or the other.

Although Tokyo enjoys an excellent transportation system, a low crime rate, and even a budget surplus, it is not a city without problems. Chief among these is the high cost of land. One square yard in Ginza now fetches more than a quarter of a million dollars. But even if a *sarariiman* (a salaried worker) manages to save that amount, he will be able to purchase only a modest two-story home located at least two hours by train from his job. Tokyo, described as lush, green, and spacious by foreign visitors in the late 19th century, is now none of these.

Right A 236-foot bronze torii (gateway) marks the entrance to Yasukuni Shrine, a sanctuary honoring soldiers, sailors, and others who have died serving Japan.

Japan's capital today is not a city of grand vistas, but of discrete and interesting places: colorful and noisy shopping streets near train stations, and quiet, restful shrine and temple grounds, not to mention nightlife offerings of a variety and quantity matched in few other cities in the world. Tokyo is not a beautiful city, but a pleasant one; not a historical city, but an impressive one; and not a perfect city, but a very livable one.

Left The small fishing village of Yokohama was opened as a port for foreign trade in 1858, after the signing of the Harris Treaty between Japan and the United States. As trade grew, so did the local communities of foreign residents. "The Bluff" area of the city is still a favored residential district of Westerners, while Chinese residents established a thriving Chinatown, now primarily a tourist spot catering to both Western and Japanese visitors.

Above *Kamakura was the political center of Japan from 1192 to 1333, and the city continued to serve as the administrative center of eastern Japan until 1573. Remaining from those bygone days are many splendid monuments, including the 37-foot Daibutsu (Great Buddha), cast in 1252.*

Left *Kamakura's Tsurugaoka Hachiman Shrine is a popular site on January 1, when people visit shrines for the first time in the new year.*

Above Seventy-five miles north of Tokyo lies Nikko, sacred precincts designated as the final resting place of the Tokugawa shoguns, who governed Japan from Edo Castle between 1600 and 1868. The tomb of the first shogun, Tokugawa Ieyasu, is located on the grounds of the most lavish mausoleum, Toshogu Shrine. The shrine is entered through a two-story, twelve-column, gabled gate called Yomeimon (Gate of Sunlight).

◆ A LANGUAGE OF COMPLEXITY AND BEAUTY ◆

The Japanese language has never been satisfactorily categorized in any of the world's main language groups. Its structure is similar to Korean, while its sounds seem to show more affinity with the Malayo-Polynesian group. Its range has been essentially limited to the nation's boundaries: all Japanese speak it and relatively few others do. The very high literacy rate of Japan has certainly contributed to the nation's economic success, while the difficulty of acquiring Japanese as a second language has likewise contributed to foreigners' historically less than satisfactory understanding of the Japanese people.

There is no archaeological evidence to indicate that the Japanese ever attempted to develop their own written language. By the time a practical need for writing arose, Japan was firmly under the cultural sway of neighboring China, and was content to use Chinese script to transcribe its own language. Although this was a natural extension of Japan's cultural and political borrowing, it was extremely unfortunate, for the Chinese language is essentially monosyllabic and lacks inflection, while Japanese is polysyllabic and highly inflected. The Chinese writing system, a set of over 40,000 simple and complex ideograms, provided a woefully cumbersome and inadequate medium through which to convey Japanese. Different methods of writing Japanese with *kanji* (Chinese characters) were tried, but the complexity of those methods ensured that writing remained a skill of scholars.

During the 9th and 10th centuries, the Chinese characters chosen to represent particular Japanese sounds were codified and abbreviated, resulting in two phonetic syllabaries called *hiragana* and *katakana*. These two systems facilitated transcription of the spoken language, contributing to the rise of a vernacular literature and, in the 11th century, the world's first novel, Lady Murasaki's *The Tale of Genji.*

Both *kana* systems, as well as *kanji*, are used in modern written Japanese. The *kanji* represent substantive words—nouns, verb stems, adjectives, and adverbs—while *hiragana* provide verb endings indicating inflection, prepositions, and other necessary grammatical markers and linking words. *Katakana* are used to transcribe foreign words, and are also employed as a script for signs and advertising. Although the regularity of the Japanese spoken language makes acquiring a rudimentary knowledge fairly easy, there is no question but that the Japanese written language is one of the most difficult in the world.

Kanji	Hiragana	Katakana	Reading
加	か	カ	ka
保	ほ	ホ	ho

Above To facilitate transcription, cumbersome kanji with sounds similar to Japanese were simplified into kana forms. Writing the kanji *cursively* resulted in hiragana, while using a portion of the character to represent the whole produced katakana.

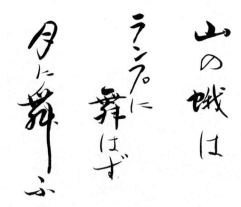

Yama no ga wa
ranpu ni mawazu
tsuki ni mau

Mountain moths do not
hover about a lamp;
they hover about the moon.

Below Although Chinese characters presented a hurdle to literature, they were a boon to pictorial art. The characters themselves were thought to possess artistic merit, and calligraphic skill was highly valued. Moreover, the brush techniques employed in writing were similar to those of painting, leading to a tradition of combining the two in narrative picture scrolls called emaki. Perhaps the finest extant emaki is this superb Heian scroll that depicts scenes from The Tale of Genji.

Above This poem, written by 20th-century poet Mizuhara Shuoshi, is in the traditional 17-syllable haiku form. The poem contains Chinese characters and both hiragana *and* katakana *forms. The first three characters in the middle line, which are written in katakana, spell the loanword* ranpu, *from the English "lamp."*

From Modern Japanese Haiku: An Anthology, *compiled and translated by* Makoto Ueda *(Toronto and Buffalo: University of Toronto Press, 1976), 152; reprinted by permission of University of Toronto Press.*

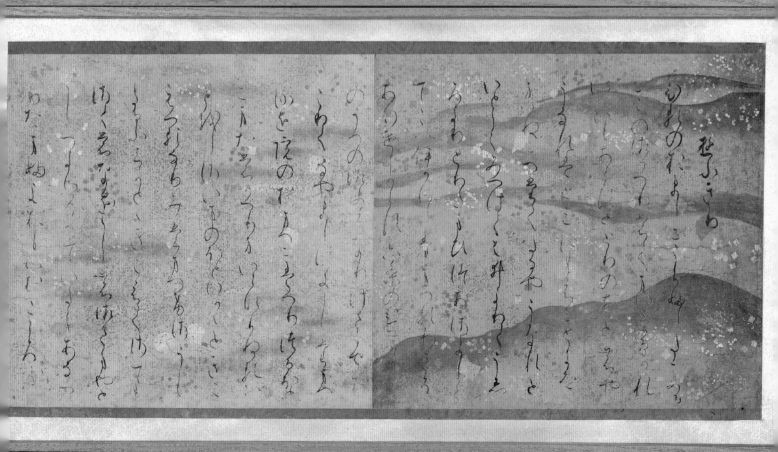

THE VARIETY OF JAPAN

Kokyō, combining the characters for old and village, means hometown. Another reading of the compound is furusato, a word commonly used on brochures promoting trips to the countryside.

ALTHOUGH JAPAN'S major tourist destinations—Tokyo, Kyoto, Nara, Nikko, and Kamakura—are readily distinguishable, smaller cities and towns have a superficial uniformity that tends to mask interesting local and regional differences. Those who have read that Japan's linguistic homogeneity has contributed to its economic success, for example, may be surprised to learn that Japanese has a number of dialects. Although many of these colloquial differences are simply pronunciation variants, others are distinct regional expressions. While Tokyoites will say irasshaimase when welcoming a guest, Kyoto residents might say oideyasu, and southerners from Okinawa, mensōre.

Various regional differences are said to distinguish Japan's two main population centers: the Kanto Plain, location of the Tokyo-Yokohama megalopolis, and the Kansai region, home to the ancient capitals of Kyoto and Nara and the bustling economic hub of Osaka. Dif-

Left   These noodles, handmade on Shodo Island in the Inland Sea, are being stretched until they reach the right thinness.

ferences between these two areas have been exacerbated by the historical shift of political and economic power from Kansai to Kanto, to the point that they have generated a gentle rivalry. Kanto people are often characterized as broad-minded and hustling, with little regard for tradition, while Kansai residents are considered as stubborn and old-fashioned. (Osaka residents have also garnered a reputation for being exceptionally tough and skillful in business.) Japanese hailing from outside these cosmopolitan centers, home to 40 percent of the population, run the risk of being labeled inaka-mono (country bumpkins).

To the Western visitor, regional differences may be most evident at mealtimes. Some variations in cuisine are subtle: Kanto foods are considered "darker," more heavily seasoned with soy sauce, while Kansai's broths of bonito flakes, salt, and seaweed are lighter, or blander, depending upon one's taste. Other differences are more obvious: Kanto sushi, for example, uses the hand-shaped rice mound familiar to patrons of sushi shops in the West, while Kansai sushi is made from rice pressed into a pan and cut into squares after the fish has been laid on top.

A traditional dish served nationwide but with great variation is nabe, a one-pot stew that incorporates regional delicacies. The Hokkaido version, Ishikari nabe, includes the salmon for which that northernmost island is famous; botan nabe, a variation served in the Kansai countryside, features wild boar, while the dote nabe of Hiroshima substitutes oysters. Other regional specialties have historical roots. Nagasaki, for centuries Japan's trading post with the outside world, is noted for its Chinese-inspired noodle dishes, while the best tofu and temple vegetarian dishes are said to be found in Kyoto, the headquarters of major Buddhist sects for more than a thousand years.

Regional products, made especially for visitors looking for gifts to take home, offer another showcase for Japanese variety. Such products not only reveal local

tastes, raw materials, and craft traditions, but also tell something of local life. From snowy Iwate Prefecture, for example, come the best *tetsubin* (iron kettles), formerly used to heat water over the open firepits of country homes. Most famous is *Nambu tetsubin*, named for the

Nambu clan that ruled the region in former days. The best *bangasa*, the lacquered paper and bamboo umbrellas featured in romantic Western portrayals of Japanese women, are made in Gifu Prefecture in central Japan. The bark of the mulberry trees that flourish there

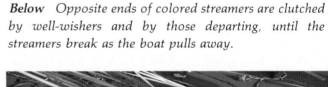

Below *A vendor selling fresh fish from the Inland Sea makes her way through a neighborhood in the seaside city of Takehara, Okayama Prefecture.*

Below *Opposite ends of colored streamers are clutched by well-wishers and by those departing, until the streamers break as the boat pulls away.*

is the material from which the *washi* paper covering the umbrellas is fashioned. Since mulberry leaves are the favored food of silkworms, both Gifu and neighboring Nagano Prefecture are also known for silk weaving, an industry that flourished there due to the area's proximity to the court in Kyoto.

Pottery also exemplifies regional variety. Connoisseurs can easily identify Hagi ware, glazed, high-fired ceramics from kilns of the city of Hagi, and Bizen ware, unglazed stoneware from Okayama Prefecture, formerly called Bizen Province. Another distinctive

Left   Morning street markets like this one at Wajima, Ishikawa Prefecture, are a thriving institution. This woman is selling dried fish, a popular snack item.

Below   The village of Shirakawa, located deep in the mountains of Gifu Prefecture, is famed for its traditional farmhouses. These houses are best known for their roofs, which are steep to prevent snow from accumulating, and expansive to allow room for raising silkworms, an industry that has long flourished in the region.

Above *Evidence of the presence of 19th-century Western residents is the Oura Catholic Church of Nagasaki, constructed in 1864. The church was built in memory of 26 martyrs crucified in Nagasaki in 1597 for refusing to give up their belief in Christianity.*

ceramic, Soma ware from Fukushima Prefecture, is readily identified by the underglaze painted design of a horse that appears on most vessels.

Kokeshi, lathe-fashioned wooden dolls, are another enduring and ubiquitous folk-art product. Although the craft dates from only the late Edo period, when relative prosperity allowed countryfolk leisure time for pursuits other than farming, these dolls are known to folk-art lovers worldwide. Since the size, shape, and decoration of each *kokeshi* identify the region where it was made, these dolls make wonderful souvenirs, the *kokeshi* of Miyagi Prefecture being especially prized.

Visitors from abroad searching for souvenirs or foods reflecting local tastes need only follow Japanese tourists, who will be doing the same thing. Japanese returning from holiday excursions invariably bring back small gifts for friends and office colleagues. Called *o-miyage*, these gifts customarily reflect something of the place visited.

Japan also offers a wealth of architectural variety. In Shitamachi, the old part of Tokyo, many Edo-period shops and houses remain, standing in contrast to the ultramodern commercial complexes being built today. And, of course, Kyoto and Nara boast splendid temples and shrines that have stood for more than a millennium. Away from these top tourist cities, however, are innumerable sights of beauty and interest. The stately homes and churches of 19th-century European residents, as well as colorful and bustling Chinatown areas, can still be seen in the old trading enclaves of Yokohama and Nagasaki. Soaring feudal castles, such as Himeji's Egret Castle, grace the skylines of provincial capitals that were once the seats of daimyo power. The Tohoku countryside is a good place to see *minka*, the traditional thatched-roof farmhouse that often served as stable, shop, and home. These elegant wooden structures themselves reflect regional diversity, since the master carpenters who built them passed on the secrets of their trade only to local apprentices.

Japanese from outlying regions, even those who have been lured to the big cities for career or other reasons, remain intensely proud of and often nostalgic about their *furusato* (hometown). Perhaps more than any other people, they remain in touch with their roots, and the same excellent transportation and communication infrastructure that keeps Japan close-knit as a nation keeps ties with hometown friends and family strong. At the start of the summer and winter holiday seasons, trains are

Left *Although today children's toys or popular souvenirs,* kokeshi *dolls may have originated as rustic memorial or funerary sculptures for honoring the spirits of the departed. Simply constructed from a single piece of hardwood,* kokeshi *feature designs and decorations that reflect the regions of their crafting.*

packed with urban residents streaming outward; they will return laden with goods and foods whose big-city equivalents they feel are less than satisfactory. And hometown partialities have a way of becoming conventional wisdom. Instead of the rivalry one might expect from such regional diversity, Japanese opinion is in surprising agreement on which prefectures grow the best rice, which make the best saké, and even which have the most beautiful women. At the same time, it seems there is no place in the country *without* a famous product. Whether the best crabs, crackers, or lacquerware, there is always something special to take home.

Below *Matsushima, literally "pine islands," is a bay containing over 260 pine-covered islets and is considered by the Japanese one of their country's three most scenic spots. Matsushima lies on the east coast near Sendai, the capital of Miyagi Prefecture and the cultural and political center of Tohoku, the northern region of Honshu.*

◈ A RICH TEXTILE TRADITION ◈

As with other facets of Japanese culture, the history of Japanese textiles has been one of adapting ideas imported from abroad, in the process creating a rich and varied tradition. Japanese textiles have been influenced by designs and techniques from China, Korea, Southeast Asia, Polynesia, and, more recently, the West; these have been modified to accord with domestic aesthetic preferences and practical needs.

Asian mainland influences are evident in *kasuri*, a woven cloth of hemp or cotton with patterns of white against a darker background. Before being dyed, certain sections of the warp and weft threads are bound tightly to exclude the dye; the patterns appear in the cloth as it is skillfully woven. *Kasuri* probably originated in India, and came to Japan via Okinawa.

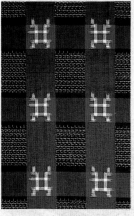

Fabrics called *shibori* employ another widespread dyeing technique of ancient origin, tie-dyeing, in which portions of the finished cloth are folded or gathered, then tied to exclude the dye. Other dyed fabrics employ paste-resist techniques, such as *tsutsugaki*, in which the resist is applied freehand, or *katazome*, which makes use of a stencil. The most widely representative of Japanese dyes is indigo, used in many parts of the world since ancient times, and in Japan from at least the early 7th century. In contrast to indigo are the bright colors of *bingata*, a stencil-dyed fabric from Okinawa that recalls the vivid patterns of fabrics from the islands of the South Pacific.

Weaving methods are also employed to produce exquisite fabrics, such as *nishiki*, an elaborate brocade that often incorporates threads of gold and silver. *Shishū* (embroidery) was used to embellish costumes for the imperial court and Noh theater, while *sashiko*, a quilting technique used to join layers of plain indigo-dyed fabric, added strength and beauty to the clothes of the common people.

kasuri

shibori

bingata

shishū

nishiki

Left A worker sorts out silkworm cocoons. As in China and Korea, the principal textile materials used in Japan were hemp and silk. The time and expense required to feed and raise the silkworms, spin threads from the cocoons, and weave the cloth made silk a fabric for the wealthy.

Right Kamakura Yoshitaro, designated a Living National Treasure, uses a stencil to apply dye-resistant paste to a fabric.

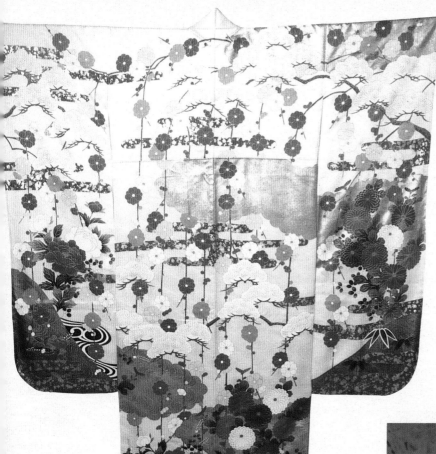

Left Creativity and craftsmanship in Japanese textiles have been supported by the value traditionally accorded elegance and propriety in dress, particularly in women's kimono and obi (below left), the broad sash that has become the kimono's focal point. The simple design of the kimono has made it a perfect canvas on which to experiment with new patterns and techniques, while the obi and other accessories are appropriate for the addition of elegant detail. Designs and motifs from nature predominate in traditional Japanese dress.

Right A man rinses dye from a piece of cloth that will become a kimono. Faintly visible in the cloth is the pattern known as komon, literally "small crests," miniature motifs repeated throughout a material. Originally used for samurai dress, the komon design (below) later became popular with Edo women and remains popular today.

RITUALS OF LIFE AND SEASON

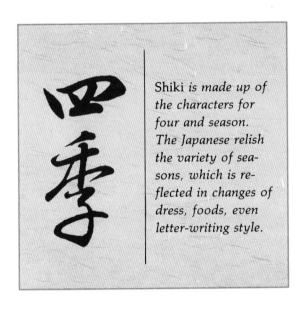

Shiki *is made up of the characters for* four *and* season. *The Japanese relish the variety of seasons, which is reflected in changes of dress, foods, even letter-writing style.*

THE YEAR in Japan unfolds as a continuum of annual occurrences, its progress clearly marked by specific seasonal events, celebrations, and holidays. Most of these temporal markers, like Setsubun, a bean-scattering ritual of purification to herald the arrival of spring, were inherited from the agricultural calendar. Others, like Shichi-Go-San, on which boys aged three and five and girls aged three and seven are taken to shrines, were established to mark life's rites of passage. Japan's 13 national holidays include observances of both types, although most, like Health-Sports Day and Culture Day, are of recent origin and lack the religious overtones of traditional celebrations. Secular and political national holidays aside, however, important events of the year are associated with the season, the weather, and the flora in bloom; they dictate plans, activities, and obligations, and are reflected in foods eaten, merchandise sold, and attire worn.

Left On the Shichi-Go-San Festival, girls of age seven and three and boys five and three are taken to shrines, where deities are thanked for watching over children.

The most important holiday and holiday season in Japan, as in all of Asia, is New Year's, which traditionally lasted two weeks and was celebrated in February, marking the arrival of spring by the old lunar calendar. Although today New Year's is fixed by the Western calendar—only January 1 is a national holiday—most businesses still close for up to a full week, allowing workers to travel to their hometowns and gather with their extended families; ancestral spirits are believed also to return to the homes of their birth at this time. New Year's is a time of renewal, a time to bring to completion the business of the old year and anticipate the work and rewards of the new. Prior to New Year's, debts are paid and greeting cards and gifts sent in appreciation of assistance received over the past year. Houses, apartments, even cars are cleaned and decorated with displays of pine, plum, and bamboo branches, symbols of longevity, constancy, and purity.

Signs of spring's arrival are evident by March, which brings Vernal Equinox Day, another national holiday, and perhaps the arrival of cherry blossoms, an eagerly awaited event. Due to Japan's great latitudinal stretch, the blooming ripples from south to north over a period of several weeks, typically appearing at the end of March in Kyushu and arriving in Hokkaido in early May. The beautiful but short-lived blossoms epitomize evanescence, and everywhere groups gather in cherry groves to admire them. It is not a sad event, however, but a spring rite celebrating life and renewal with unabashed revelry, drinking, and song. April 29, which formerly celebrated Emperor Hirohito's birthday, was designated Greenery Day upon his death in 1989. It is the first of the three national holidays, along with Constitution Day on May 3 and Children's Day on May 5, that make up what is popularly known as Golden Week. May 4 is also customarily a holiday, allowing vacations during the fine weather that precedes the rainy season.

Spring is the season for several milestones in the lives of young people. In February comes the culmination of

Above New Year's celebrations include hatsumōde, *the year's first visit to a shrine or temple. Often wearing kimono, people pray for good fortune for the new year.*

Above right *About to greet guests at her wedding reception, a bride wears a gorgeous kimono. At the wedding ceremony, she wore a white kimono, symbolic of the purity of the ritual, carried out in the presence of Shinto gods.*

Below *All over rural Japan, spring rice-planting ceremonies, such as this one at Mibu, Hiroshima Prefecture, are important occasions on the annual calendar.*

Right *Although it occurs during the spring rainy season, iris-viewing is a popular event. To the Japanese, flowers like the iris and the hydrangea are most beautiful when viewed in the rain.*

Opposite middle right *Children dressed in light, cotton kimono called* yukata *enjoy playing with fireworks at a neighborhood summer festival.*

so-called "examination hell," nationwide testing for entry into universities, in Japan more than anywhere else a crucial determinant of job and career. Spring is also the season for graduation and job-hunting, although important corporate employers will have signed students from top universities as early as the previous summer (in spite of government guidelines designed to discourage this practice). Recruits will report en masse to spring indoctrination programs, the typical start of a lifetime career with the same firm. As in the West, spring is also the time for marriage. On weekends and especially on days deemed lucky by the traditional fortune calendar, wedding halls will be fully booked. The marriage ceremony, usually conducted under Shinto auspices, will be followed by a dinner reception in a package deal that will cost about $10,000 for a modest party of 50 guests.

Celebration of seasonal flora is not restricted to cherry-blossom viewing, but is popular from late winter through fall. Especially appreciated are plum blossoms, symbolizing fortitude for their ability to bloom in the harsh cold of February; irises, whose large purple or blue blossoms brighten the rainy season of June to mid-July; and September's chrysanthemums, revered as emblems of the imperial family. At these times, visitors flock to

Right At a study retreat in the mountains, students suffer through the rigors of "examination hell," the endless study required to pass tests for entrance to high school and college.

temples, shrines, and gardens noted for their seasonal plantings. In the fall, trips are arranged to the countryside to view the changing colors of the leaves, particularly the brilliant yellow of ginkgoes and the fiery red of maples against the green pines.

Central to the annual cycle of observances are *matsuri*, the celebrations of local shrines and their communities. These are mainly of sacred origin, established to propitiate those deities whose benevolence can assure abundant harvests and the welfare of the community. *Matsuri* are essentially acts of communion, both among community members and between them and the tutelary deities of local shrines. The larger urban *matsuri* may often appear more like commercial festivals than religious rites, but these too are in keeping with Japanese attitudes toward the spirits, who are to be entertained as well as revered. Many *matsuri* include a ritual perambulation about the neighborhood by the shrine deities, who ride in portable shrines called *mikoshi*. These are borne on the shoulders of organized, chanting groups who have practiced hard for the annual events.

Although there is likely no day in the year when a local festival is not under way somewhere in Japan, late spring can be considered to herald the festival season, for it is from then through early fall when most of the major festivals are celebrated. These include the three big festivals of Tokyo—the Kanda, Sanja, and Sanno *matsuri*—held between mid-May and mid-June, and the many August observances of O-bon, during which ancestral spirits are again believed to return to the homes of their birth. Although of Buddhist origin, and thus imported from mainland Asia, O-bon accorded with the traditional belief in twice yearly visits by the departed, and though it includes no national holiday, O-bon remains one of the three important holiday seasons of the year. Again, most workplaces close from several days to a week to allow hometown visits, and gifts and cards are exchanged. O-bon celebrations conclude with bonfires or lanterns floated on waterways, to guide the spirit visitors back to the netherworld. As the rites of Shinto normally formalize Japanese marriages, so are the services of Buddhism, with its deities of infinite compassion and concept of karmic rebirth, deemed appropriate for funerals. Memorial services will be held at fixed intervals, and grave sites regularly cleaned and swept for the comfort of the departed. Death is an accepted event in the cycle of individual life; the life of the family continues.

Even more than in the West, holidays and seasonal events in modern Japan have become linked with commercial interests. Both New Year's and O-bon celebrations follow periods of customary semiannual bonus payments, making holiday spending for gift-giving and visits home less difficult. Ever alert to opportunities, business interests have also encouraged the incorporation of popular Western holidays into the annual calendar. Valentine's Day is celebrated, but with a Japanese twist—women buy chocolates for the men in their lives. (March 14's "White Day," on which men are expected to reciprocate, has not proven as successful.) Ginza window-shoppers in December can view scenes of the Nativity or Santa in his workshop, and Kentucky Fried Chicken has managed to establish itself as "traditional" Christmas Eve fare. The intrusion of blatant commer-

cialism, however, has never become a controversial issue, for ritual giving and spending, motivated by either affection or obligation, accord with custom. Japanese love a celebration, and the pressures of increasingly urbanized and Westernized lifestyles seem only to have enhanced the enthusiasm with which they participate in the national calendar of both traditional and modern rites of life and season.

Below A man places incense sticks in an urn at Ishiteji, a temple in Matsuyama. Fanning smoke from the incense onto a body part is supposed to protect that part from illness or injury.

Japanese dwellings have traditionally reflected Japanese attitudes toward nature. They have been designed not to exclude nature, but to harmonize with it; not to isolate residents from the natural elements, but to incorporate those elements in a comfortable living environment.

Japan's population centers historically were located in areas that enjoyed cold but short, dry winters; house design was focused on comfort during the long, sultry summers. The basic design that evolved shows strong Polynesian influences, with a raised living area that allowed air to circulate freely. Roofs had extended eaves, protecting the open structures from sun and rain. Except for the sometimes high and elaborate roof, architectural elements tended to be horizontal and minimal.

Japanese have historically shared the Chinese preference for wood as a building material for the abodes of men and gods. Temples, shrines, and dwellings were built of wood, while stone was reserved for walls, fortifications, and funerary structures. Wood is pliant and remains cooler than stone in the summer, and single-story wooden dwellings are earthquake resistant, an important consideration in Japan.

Although relatively few older homes remain, especially in large cities, elements of the traditional house are found in modern houses and apartments. Most have at least one tatami room, which often features a *tokonoma*, a decorative alcove, and most still divide interior space with sliding wood-framed paper doors called *fusuma*.

Even though the high cost of land has pared the garden areas of city homes to a minimum, most retain a few feet for planting between the house and the wall surrounding the property; a garden view can thus still be enjoyed through the windows, which are now more commonly Western style.

Left *The top roof of this traditional farmhouse is made of thatch, while the lower one is made of slate.*

Below *The pleasing visual proportions of the interior are achieved by using dimensions that are of a standard unit called a* ken, *approximately six feet. The distance between supporting posts and the dimensions of doors and tatami flooring all reflect this basic unit. Use of* fusuma *allows living space to be readily adjusted.*

Above left The traditional dwelling compound encompasses a living area and garden, surrounded by a wall and gate marking the transition from public to private space. Visitors remove their shoes at a covered entryway called a genkan *before stepping up into the house.*

Above right Futon (traditional bedding) is laid out at night, then folded and stored away during the day to free space for other uses.

Left *The ceremonial focal point of the house is the* tokonoma, *a small alcove that typically features a hanging scroll and flower arrangement reflecting the season. When a meal is served in this room, the guest of honor is seated closest to the* tokonoma. *The* tokonoma *is attached to the* tokobashira, *a supporting post of exquisite wood that is considered the ritual "pillar" of the house.*

Below *Sliding latticed doors called* shōji *open to the outside to bring nature inside. Garden views may be enjoyed from within or from the* engawa, *a narrow veranda running along the sides of the house.*

THE JAPANESE AT PLAY

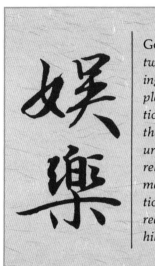

Goraku *combines two characters meaning pleasure, one the pleasure of conversation with women, the other the pleasure of music and relaxation. Goraku means any recreational pastime, from reading a book to hiking.*

UNTIL RECENTLY, stereotypes of the Japanese most prevalent in the West were those of the "economic animal": uniformed factory workers or blue-suited businessmen who lived in cramped suburban high-rises or company housing, commuted on packed rush-hour trains, and spent long and tedious hours on the job. These were images that accorded with our acknowledgment of Japan's position as a new economic giant; only a tireless and dedicated work force could attain such success in world markets. Moreover, they were images supported by statistical evidence: Japanese work more hours per year (2,044 hours in 1990) than do Americans or British (1,900 hours) or Germans or French (1,600 hours), and take far fewer vacation days.

Today, however, a new portrait of the Japanese is gaining currency, that of globetrotting, freespending holidaymakers. And the new stereotype has equally impressive statistical support: more than 25,000 Japanese

---

Left High school students in central Tokyo practice baseball, introduced into Japan in 1873 and today the most popular sport in the nation.

tourists arrive every *week* in Hawaii, each spending an average of five times as much as their counterparts from the U.S. mainland, totaling an estimated $825 million annually. These are the Japanese we meet in our own countries, emerging from first-class hotels, strolling through shopping districts, and snapping photos of famous sights. Their preferred leisure pursuits appear similar to ours: shopping and sightseeing, golf, tennis, and skiing.

This short list, however, while valid, detracts from both the diversity of Japanese leisure activities and the intensity with which Japanese pursue them. As in other areas of modern Japanese life, this diversity seems to derive from an ingrained and fearless eclecticism. The list of leisure and recreational activities in Japan is probably longer than anywhere else in the world, for it is the sum of the new and imported incorporated willy-nilly into the traditional and indigenous, without the latter being supplanted or abandoned. A typical young woman will likely be taking both tea-ceremony and tennis lessons; a young man may belong both to a windsurfing club and a group that bears the *mikoshi* (portable shrine) in neighborhood festivals. Both the Kokugikan (National Sumo Stadium) and Tokyo Dome (home of the Tokyo Giants baseball team) regularly attract sellout crowds; a theater evening might take in a Noh play or Shakespeare (in either Japanese or English); an ordinary night out might include hitting a few buckets of balls at a rooftop driving range, a meal at a Thai restaurant, and a disco; stay-at-homes might choose from a samurai drama, Wagnerian opera, or "The Cosby Show" on TV. The point is not that any of these activities is unavailable in other countries, but that they cannot all, at all times, be assumed as leisure-time possibilities. Kabuki in New York is rare; a Broadway musical in Tokyo is not.

Of course, it is the enormous wealth created by the Japanese in the postwar period that has allowed them, for the first time, to reveal themselves to the West as lovers of leisure and fun. However, the truth of the matter is not simply that having suddenly become rich, they

have suddenly become hedonists; Japanese have always gone about enjoying themselves with surprising intensity. The Shinto religion has no proscriptions on excess merriment; on the contrary, it encourages celebration as much as reverence. This is attested to by the boisterous proceedings of local festivals and the revelry of other seasonal events, from cherry-blossom viewing to December's *bōnenkai*, literally a "forget-the-year party."

A clue to the Japanese approach to life is offered in the commonly heard phrase *Ganbatte!*—an exhortation to "hang in there!" It bespeaks an outlook that presupposes life to indeed be difficult, but manageable through patience and hard work. Every task completed or passage of life weathered calls for a celebration to mark it. Even ordinary workdays are often concluded with drinking sessions or some other form of relaxation. The narrow side streets surrounding train stations are typically crammed with small businesses offering a wide variety of leisure pursuits—movie theaters and restaurants of all types, gamerooms for mahjong and *pachinko* (a pinball-type arcade game), and bars featuring sympathetic hostesses or *karaoke* equipment for sing-alongs.

If this description seems at variance with stereotypes of "workaholic" Japanese, perhaps a basic assumption of outside observers is at fault; the Japanese may be applying themselves diligently not only to work, as is sup-

posed, but also to life. Indeed, the Japanese take their fun seriously. One doesn't just play golf, for example; one reads books on the subject, studies the game in classes, watches tournaments on TV, and practices in the street in front of one's home (or, always surprising to foreign visitors, on train platforms).

The first ride on a resort-bound train with Japanese holidaymakers is always a revelation for those who have previously ridden only on commuter lines. Passengers who would normally be quietly reading magazines or listening to English language-study tapes are chatting loudly while munching on an elaborate spread of snacks, washed down with beer or whiskey and water. This marks the beginning of a Japanese vacation, which will adhere to the rigorous schedule for which group tours are especially notorious. A typical Japanese vacation, especially to a foreign destination, may be relatively short by Western standards, but to compensate, not a moment will be wasted. Major sights will be taken in and local cuisines sampled, with time carefully allocated for everything from shopping to group photo sessions. The return flight may arrive just in time for the ex-vacationers to get a few hours of rest before rising for work the following morning, but a good time will have been had by all. These days *Ganbatte!* is heard on Hawaiian beaches and Hokkaido ski slopes as well as in the office.

Left The advent of spring is celebrated with hanami, gatherings to enjoy the blossoming cherry trees, here in Tokyo's Koganei Park.

Right Today a venerable and respected dramatic art whose roles are played by men, Kabuki originated with the performances of an all-female troupe in Kyoto in the early 17th century. The leader of that original group was a shrine dancer named Okuni, and her outdoor musical entertainments were considered less than respectable.

Below The stately art of Noh reflects the Japanese appreciation of suggestion rather than realistic portrayal. While its origins have been traced to such diverse sources as dance, acrobatics, and magic acts imported from China in the 7th century, Noh became established only in the 14th century when the performances of Kan'ami (1333–1384) and his son Zeami (1363–1443) captured the attention of the shogun.

Above There are over 2,000 hot springs throughout the Japanese islands, and a trip to an onsen (hot springs) is a popular excursion. The waters are believed by many to offer a variety of health benefits; others frequent onsen simply to relax and enjoy the scenery, especially the fall and winter views from a rustic rotemburo (outdoor bath).

Left After-hours socializing takes place in bars serving food, such as this yakitoriya, whose specialty is bites of chicken grilled and served on skewers. Before it is grilled, the chicken is either sprinkled with salt or dipped in a thick, sweet sauce.

Right Since playing golf is viewed as a key to good business relations and a mark of status as well as a pleasant outdoor sport, Japanese golfers take their game very seriously. The prohibitive price of club memberships and greens fees makes practice at driving ranges a popular pastime.

Below On October 10, Health-Sports Day, athletic events are held to emphasize the importance of physical education. In Chiba Prefecture, 16,000 Nomura employees and family members have gathered from all parts of Japan to participate in the investment group's annual outdoor meet.

◆ THE WAY OF THE WARRIOR ◆

The development of Japanese martial arts is strongly connected with the rise of the samurai in the 11th and 12th centuries, when two great noble houses were contending for supremacy. Ultimately, the Minamoto clan defeated the Taira clan and set up the first shogunate, or military governorship, at Kamakura. This marked the beginning of a feudal age in which the samurai, like the knights of Europe, formed a class of professional warriors. The samurai class was not disbanded until the mid-1870s.

In early feudal Japan, samurai studied what were referred to as the *bugei jūhappan*, literally "18 martial arts." These included the mastery of skills and weapons familiar in the West—archery and horsemanship, dirk and halberd—as well as others distinctly Japanese, such as needle spitting. Included also was *ninjutsu*, a complete system of infiltration and assassination that has recently commanded popular attention in the West. During the relatively peaceful Edo period that followed the reunification of Japan in 1603, the martial-arts canon was pared to seven: swordsmanship, spearmanship, horseback riding, archery, judo, skill with firearms, and military strategy. Together, these were taught as *bushidō*, or the "way of the warrior."

There is much more to *bushidō*, however, than practical combat skills. The study of martial arts in Japan has traditionally been linked with spiritual training, in accordance especially with the precepts of Confucianism and Zen Buddhism. From the former came the identification of the martial way with the ethical way, and the exaltation of loyalty and obligation as cardinal virtues. From the latter came the rationale and techniques of meditation needed for physical and spiritual preparation. These included honing concentration to the point that pain and fear could be ignored, and attaining insight into the false duality that makes life appear more desirable than death. The true samurai held belief more valuable than technique, insight more important than action. The way of the warrior was a way of life, and he who had mastered it was at peace with himself and in harmony with his environment.

Kyudo

Kyudo, the "way of the bow," owes more to civil archery, which prescribed shooting from a standing position, than to military archery, which was chiefly an equestrian martial art. Kyudo's emphasis on concentration, form, and etiquette stems from its strong association with Confucian ethics and Zen.

Sumo

Sumo is a form of wrestling originally devised for the entertainment of townspeople and Shinto deities on festival days; later its techniques were adapted and refined by samurai, to be used as a last resort on the battlefield. Sumo today is a widely followed spectator sport, with its champions as popular in Japan as soccer and football heroes are in the West.

Judo

Literally the "way of softness," judo is a form of unarmed combat that stresses speed, coordination, and agility over physical strength. Judo techniques are designed to allow a weaker adversary to absorb and nullify a

stronger opponent's charge, using the force of the attack to overcome the aggressor.

Aikido

Aikido was derived from the unarmed martial art of self-defense known as jujutsu, which was imported from the Asian continent in ancient times. Like judo, aikido takes advantage of the force of an attack, employing a variety of holds and grips to redirect that force, toppling and defeating the attacker.

Karate

Karate, meaning "empty hand," is a form of unarmed combat that was practiced in China in ancient times, later entering Japan through Okinawa. Although technically an art of self-defense, karate employs a variety of fast and powerful strikes, thrusts, and kicks to subdue opponents.

Kendo

Samurai training with the two-handed sword led to the development of kendo, the "way of the sword." Although sword skills became less in demand with the peace of the Edo period, kendo survived due to its strong moral and spiritual elements; it was regarded as a way of life as much as a martial art.

INTO THE 21ST CENTURY

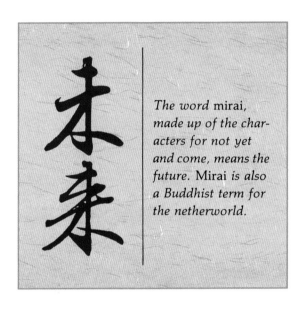

The word mirai, *made up of the characters for* not yet *and* come, *means the future.* Mirai *is also a Buddhist term for the netherworld.*

IT IS ODD that Westerners tend to view Japan as conservative, intractable, and unchanging, for it has undergone more wrenching transformations in its culture and institutions than most other nations, and modern Japan can certainly be described as dynamic and progressive. A close look today, 50 years ago, and 100 years ago reveals three very different Japans, and the nation continues to remake itself at a remarkable speed.

The pace of this change sharpens generational differences in attitudes toward work, marriage, and lifestyle. Children, taller than their parents due to a postwar diet higher in protein, vex their elders by being unimpressed with many traditional values. Japanese of the so-called *shinjinrui*, the "new breed," prefer to vacation abroad rather than sweep ancestral graves during the summer holidays, and to go skiing rather than gather with the family over New Year's. The high cost of urban real estate, coupled with the value only recently placed

Left Disgruntled citizens march in a May Day demonstration against government officials accused of accepting bribes from big-business concerns.

on privacy and independence, has led to a decline in the custom of extended families living together; modern newlyweds rent apartments away from both sets of parents. Wives today may choose to work after children are born; husbands may spurn the security of lifetime employment and change jobs for such nontraditional reasons as higher pay. Young men leave the farm and head for the bright lights of Tokyo. Young women do too, in even greater numbers, creating a shortage of eligible brides in the countryside.

In Tokyo, politicians face on the one side demands by the West to increase imports of agricultural products, and on the other side opposition to market-opening policies by farmers, the ruling party's main constituency. These leaders worry about declining savings rates, the "graying society" (by the year 2000, 20 percent of Japanese will be over 60 years of age), and land prices so high that a burial plot in Tokyo a mere 21 feet square could easily cost $150,000.

To be sure, Japan has problems, some similar to those of other nations, others peculiarly Japanese. Chief among these is the task of determining Japan's role in the modern world, its position among and relationship with other countries. Japan's current economic stature is unprecedented in the history of nations, for it has been attained without territorial expansion and attendant widening political control. Japan did, of course, initially attempt to gain power through conquest, but it embarked upon that ill-fated campaign at a time when imperialism was no longer tolerated as a path to greatness. Defeated and destroyed in World War II, Japan harnessed the talent and energy of its people to achieve greatness according to the new rules of peaceful international commerce. Although impoverished in land and resources, it nevertheless succeeded beyond all reasonable expectations, creating the world's most productive economy on a per capita basis, and, simultaneously, the contradictions that characterize its position today: a country militarily insignificant and politically inexperienced in

the international arena, yet one widely resented and feared. Although Japan's security is assured by the presence of U.S. troops, many Americans consider Japan the greatest threat to their own security.

These contradictions must be understood by both Japan and the West if future relations are to remain amicable. Yet misinterpretations of the Japanese and their motives continue to be voiced, not only by politicians playing to their constituencies but also by journalists and academics who should know better. One theory holds that Japan's economic ascendancy is simply an extension of World War II by conquest through trade rather than weaponry, and suggests the need for military or economic containment. It is a theory with a particularly odious corollary, that the Japanese are a race of extremists, incapable of the moderation required to be contributing equals with citizens of other countries.

Another charge often leveled against Japan is that it has been able to surge ahead economically due to the "free ride" afforded by American military protection. But the obvious solution—to encourage Japan to undertake its own defense—is rejected for fear of creating a new Asian military superpower, one whose views have too often not accorded with those of its neighbors. This fear is seldom explicitly stated—though in 1990 the top U.S. Marine Corps general in Japan was sacked for suggesting to the *Washington Post* that its watchdog role was the chief reason for continuing U.S. military presence in Japan—but it continues to color and confuse policy.

There is no question of Japan's aspirations to the leadership of Asia, for it is actively wooing its neighbors by providing them assistance and support. Since the mid-'80s, Japanese imports of manufactured goods from Hong Kong, Singapore, Taiwan, and Korea have increased by 20 percent annually, while Japanese aid to ASEAN countries runs six times that of the U.S. Organizations such as MITI's New Asian Industries Development Plan and the ASEAN Japan Development Bank have been established to promote and coordinate aid, trade, and investment. Still, Japanese assistance is often criticized as exploitative and self-serving, while the integration of Asian

---

Above *Public housing, typically uniform and utilitarian, is nonetheless highly sought after as private housing becomes increasingly unaffordable.*

Middle *The role of the Self-Defense Force is problematic for a nation that has renounced war.*

Below *Increasing numbers of foreigners seeking work in Japan, shown here receiving visa-application forms from immigration officials, have given rise to pressing new social issues.*

economies under Japan's aegis is feared by many in the West.

Given such difficulties, is there hope for optimism regarding Japan's relations with the West? Yes, because cooler heads in world capitals understand that balanced and amicable relations among the three economic superpowers—the U.S., Japan, and the European Community—are essential for world stability in the 21st century. Efforts are being made in Japan to alter structural and institutional characteristics that give rise to charges of unfairness, to create a more open Japan. Moreover, when the problems besetting the relationship are examined, it is seen that the drive to resolve them stems from a shared objective—attaining for Japan a position of influence and authority commensurate with the ability of the Japanese to contribute to a better world. And Japan, a nation of fabulous wealth and magnificent cultural accomplishments, stands as eloquent testimony that its citizens have much to contribute.

Below *With the completion of the Seto Ohashi bridge connecting Honshu and Shikoku, the four main islands of Japan were linked by surface transportation.*

❖ A VISUAL FEAST ❖

Japanese foods clearly mirror the origins, development, and characteristics of Japanese culture. Central to the cuisine are the traditional ingredients of rice, fish, and soybeans. Since remote antiquity, when wet-rice cultivation was brought from the mainland, rice has occupied a revered position, and its seasonal cycle has dictated the rhythm and rituals of Japanese life. Combined with local vegetables and fruits, rice provided simple but adequate sustenance. For oils and proteins, the Japanese relied on foods from the sea, with which the waters surrounding the islands have always been abundantly blessed.

The powerful influence of China during the 7th and 8th centuries brought both Buddhism, which proscribed eating the flesh of four-legged animals, and soybeans, which conveniently provided a high-protein substitute. The Japanese did not begin to eat pork and beef until the mid-19th century, when the country opened up to the West. Soybeans have remained an essential ingredient in Japanese cooking in the form of tofu, or bean curd, *miso* (a bean paste used mostly in soups), and, of course, soy sauce. Throughout its history, Japan has continued to borrow and assimilate ingredients and cooking styles from the outside, always adapting them to satisfy the preferences of the Japanese palate. Noodles came from China, a Portuguese cooking style led to tempura, and beef introduced from the West was cooked Japanese style to make sukiyaki.

Aside from its eclecticism, Japanese cuisine exhibits two other hallmarks of Japanese aesthetics: attention to season and emphasis on presentation. Japanese have not, for the most part, been attracted to the conveniences of frozen foods, preferring their traditional ways of buying and serving whatever is in season. These foods are served in small portions in a wide variety of dishes, offering a pleasing display of both complementary and contrasting shapes, colors, and textures. No cuisine in the world places more emphasis on the seasonal appropriateness of ingredients and the visual appeal of food.

Despite the availability today of cuisines from all nations, traditional foods not only remain popular in Japan but, due to their attractiveness and health benefits, have found a new following in the West. The long life expectancy of the Japanese attests to the fact that the traditional Japanese diet is nutritious and well-rounded. Shown here (clockwise from the upper right) are udon, thick wheat noodles that are served in a variety of ways, here offered with tempura; soba, a thinner buckwheat noodle, here served cold on a bamboo tray with dipping sauce; a simple meal of shōjin ryōri, vegetarian fare served at temples; eki-ben, a box lunch sold in train stations for eating on board; a flask and cups for serving saké; and sushi, raw fish served on bite-size beds of vinegared rice.

This dinner at a traditional Japanese inn includes (clockwise from the upper left) grilled seafood, tempura, watermelon, boiled prawns and vegetables, clear soup, appetizers, broiled fish, and salad. In the center is an assortment of sashimi, slices of raw fish. Such meals typically include specialties of the region and the season; the presence of watermelon indicates it is summer.

The Publisher would like to thank the following for permission to reproduce various art objects: Chino City Togariishi Archaeological Museum 19 (*Venus of Jomon*); Gotoh Museum 46–47 (*Tale of Genji Scroll*); Ii Naoyoshi 18 (*Battle of Sekigahara Screen*); Imperial Household Agency 19 (portrait of Prince Shotoku and sons, *Nanban Screen*); Jingoji 19 (portrait of Minamoto no Yoritomo); Nezu Institute of Fine Arts 36 (*Iris Screens*); Tokyo National Museum 18 (*Rain at Shono*), 19 (Yayoi pottery, *Murasaki Shikibu's Diary Scroll*), 37 (teabowl "Amadera," *Haboku Landscape*, lacquer box).

The Publisher also thanks the Uno family for graciously allowing interior photographs to be taken of the Uno house.

Other photo credits: Hibi Sadao 18 (*Battle of Sekigahara Screen*); J.O. Photo Agency 27 (below), 30 (below), 38, 67 (above); Mainichi Newspapers 18 (atomic bomb); Douglas McNamee 40 (below), 59 (below); Meikyo Katsuo 46–47 (*Tale of Genji Scroll*); Ogano Minoru 22 (below), 76 (sushi, saké flask, *soba*).

Captions

p. 1 (half title) Weeping cherries, Heian Shrine, Kyoto.
pp. 2-3 (title page) Terraced rice fields, Saga Prefecture.
pp. 4-5 (Contents) Carp streamers, Gunma Prefecture.
p. 6 (opposite Foreword) Path to Fushimi Inari Shrine, Kyoto.
pp. 8-9 Boat on the Katsura River, Arashiyama, Kyoto.
p. 78 Fish and octopus, Okayama Prefecture.
p. 80 Temple bell, Iwate Prefecture.

ABOUT THE PHOTOGRAPHERS

(Listed alphabetically by surname)

Torin Boyd, born in Pennsylvania in 1960, began his career photographing surfers. Upon graduation from photography school, he worked as a newspaper photographer before moving to Tokyo in 1986. Mr. Boyd specializes in images of modern Japan, and has done work for *U.S. News & World Report, Fortune, Forbes,* and other magazines and book publishers.

16 (above left), 18 (Natsume), 23 (above), 40 (above), 41 (below), 43, 56, 60–61, 69 (below), 72, 74 (all), 75, 76 (*shōjin ryōri*).

Neil Krivonak, born in Colorado in 1963, photographs a wide range of subjects. His images have appeared in numerous magazines, and he has worked for such clients as Coca-Cola, Motorola, and Boeing. Mr. Krivonak is best known for his photographs of people, including Prince Charles and Whitney Houston. A world traveler, he has photographed in Hong Kong, New Zealand, Thailand, Alaska, and Europe.

16 (below), 42 (below), 58 (above right), 62 (below), 63 (all), 64, 68 (below), 70 (above, below).

Frank Leather, born in London in 1946, has resided in Kyoto since 1980. His photographs have appeared in numerous books, including *Mishima by Canales, Buddhist Festivals,* and *Festivals and Celebrations.* A constant traveler, Mr. Leather has captured images of China, the Far East, the Middle East, and Europe.

1, 20, 26 (below left), 27 (above left), 54 (*shishū*).

Morita Toshitaka was born in Osaka in 1946. A specialist in photographing natural scenery, Mr. Morita has had his works published in numerous books, including *Nihon Kokuritsu Koen* (Japan's National Parks), *Setouchi* (The Inland Sea), and *Nihon Retto Hana Hyakkei* (One Hundred Floral Views of Japan).

8-9, 11 (Hokkaido, Wakayama, Ehime), 14, 15 (Kobe, Nagano), 16 (above right), 22 (above), 24–25, 26 (right), 28, 30 (above), 32–33, 34 (above), 35, 44 (right), 45, 50 (below right), 51, 53.

Sato Norio, born in Tochigi Prefecture in 1940, is known for his photographs of Buddhist art and objects from Japanese history and folklore. His photography has appeared in various books, including *Minwa to Densetsu* (Folk Tales and Legends) and *Fudoki* (Japanese Prefectural Topography).

27 (bell), 54 (*kasuri, bingata,* stenciler), 67 (below), 71 (all), 76 (*udon*), 77.

Tomita Hiroyuki was born in Fukuoka Prefecture in 1958. Inspired by the traditional homes of his birthplace, Tomita began photographing Tokyo's old Shitamachi districts. The result was his book *Soko no Machikado* (Street Corners). Today Tomita continues to turn his lens on Shitamachi, in particular its puppet and brush makers and other traditional craftsmen, as well as Tokyo's many rivers.

17, 41 (above), 42 (above), 50 (below left), 54 (*shibori, nishiki*), 55 (kimono, *obi*), 68 (above), 78, 80.

Yasuda Narumi, born in Kagawa Prefecture in 1947, specializes in trains, landscapes, and Japanese festivals. Mr. Yasuda's works have appeared in numerous magazines, calendars, and other publications, including *Michinoku Bojo* (Journey into Northern Japan) and *Furusato no Shiki o Yuku: Nihon no Joki-Kikansha* (Steam Locomotives Through the Japanese Countryside).

2-3, 4-5, 6, 10, 11 (Yamagata, Nagano, Miyagi, Tottori, Kyushu), 12, 15 (Kyushu, Hokkaido), 23 (below), 26 (above left), 27 (above right), 31 (above, below), 34 (below), 44 (above left, below left), 48, 50 (above), 52 (above, below), 54 (dyer, silk cocoons, weaver), 55 (*komon,* below right), 58 (above left, below), 59 (above, middle), 62 (above), 66, 69 (above), 76 (*ekiben*).